Inside Social Media Algorithms: Breaking Down How Platforms Work and the Influence of Algorithms on Our Lives

James Relington

DEDICATION

To all the users navigating the digital landscape, questioning what they see, and seeking to understand the invisible forces shaping their online experiences. This book is dedicated to those who value truth over virality, critical thinking over convenience, and human connection over algorithmic manipulation. May we all continue to challenge, learn, and reclaim control over the technology that influences our lives every day.

AKNOWLEDGEMENTS

I would like to express my deepest gratitude to everyone who contributed to the creation of this book. To my colleagues and mentors, your insights and expertise have been invaluable. To the organizations and professionals who shared their experiences and best practices, your contributions have enriched this work. A special thank you to my family and friends for their unwavering support and encouragement throughout this journey.

The Rise of Social Media Algorithms

Social media has transformed from a simple tool for connecting with friends and family to a powerful force shaping global communication, culture, and even political landscapes. At the heart of this transformation lies a crucial but often misunderstood element: algorithms. These complex systems determine what users see, when they see it, and how they engage with content. In the early days of social media, platforms displayed posts in chronological order, offering users a straightforward experience where the most recent content appeared first. However, as platforms grew and content became overwhelming, chronological feeds were replaced by algorithm-driven curation designed to enhance engagement and keep users on the platform longer.

The shift toward algorithmic feeds was not just a technological advancement but also a business decision. Social media companies quickly realized that engagement was the key to their success, and the best way to maximize engagement was by showing users the most relevant and compelling content based on their behavior. The introduction of machine learning and artificial intelligence allowed these platforms to track user activity, analyze preferences, and predict what content would generate the highest level of interaction. The goal was simple: keep users scrolling, clicking, and engaging for as long as possible.

Facebook was one of the first major platforms to fully embrace algorithm-driven content distribution. By prioritizing posts from friends and family over public pages, the platform ensured that users saw content that resonated with them emotionally. This strategy increased user retention and interaction, making Facebook an even more integral part of people's daily lives. Twitter and Instagram soon followed, shifting from chronological timelines to algorithmic ranking systems that personalized each user's feed. The rise of personalized feeds led to significant improvements in user engagement, but it also sparked criticism regarding transparency and fairness.

One of the most significant turning points in the evolution of social media algorithms was the introduction of engagement-based ranking. Instead of simply showing users the most recent posts, platforms began ranking content based on likes, shares, comments, and watch time. This change amplified the visibility of highly engaging posts, often leading to the rapid spread of viral content. While this system helped surface entertaining and relevant material, it also had unintended consequences, such as the spread of misinformation and sensationalism. Content that provoked strong emotional reactions—whether positive or negative—tended to receive more engagement, leading algorithms to favor extreme or controversial viewpoints over balanced and informative content.

The dominance of engagement-based algorithms fundamentally changed how people consumed news and information. Traditional media outlets had to adapt their strategies to remain relevant in an algorithm-driven landscape. Clickbait headlines, sensational stories, and emotionally charged content became more common as publishers sought to maximize their reach. The prioritization of engagement over accuracy also led to the rise of misinformation, with false or misleading content often outperforming factual reporting due to its emotionally provocative nature.

Another major shift occurred with the rise of recommendation algorithms. Platforms like YouTube, TikTok, and Instagram Reels took personalization to the next level by curating content based on user behavior rather than social connections. Instead of simply displaying posts from people a user followed, these platforms analyzed watch history, interactions, and browsing patterns to recommend content from a wide range of creators. This approach introduced users to new voices and perspectives but also created concerns about filter bubbles and echo chambers, where individuals were increasingly exposed to content that reinforced their existing beliefs while minimizing exposure to opposing viewpoints.

TikTok became one of the most successful platforms to leverage recommendation algorithms. Unlike traditional social networks, TikTok's For You Page does not rely on a user's existing network but instead serves content purely based on engagement metrics and viewing habits. This strategy enabled the rapid rise of viral trends and made TikTok one of the most addictive social media platforms. The effectiveness of TikTok's algorithm-driven content delivery model influenced competitors, leading to the introduction of similar features on other platforms, such as Instagram Reels and YouTube Shorts.

The economic incentives behind social media algorithms cannot be overlooked. Platforms generate revenue primarily through advertising, and the longer users stay engaged, the more ads they see. This financial model encourages companies to refine their algorithms to maximize user retention. The introduction of AI-driven personalization has made platforms even more efficient at predicting user behavior, increasing the time spent on social media and, consequently, advertising revenue. However, this model has also raised ethical concerns regarding privacy, data collection, and the potential for manipulation.

As algorithms became more sophisticated, they started to influence not only content discovery but also user behavior. Studies have shown that social media algorithms can shape opinions, influence emotions, and even impact mental health. By prioritizing content that triggers strong emotional reactions, algorithms can create an addictive feedback loop where users seek more stimulation, leading to increased screen time and, in some cases, negative psychological effects such as anxiety and depression. The influence of algorithms extends beyond entertainment and personal interactions, affecting politics, public discourse, and even democratic processes.

Despite their widespread use, social media algorithms remain largely opaque to the general public. While platforms occasionally provide insights into how their ranking systems work, the exact mechanisms behind algorithmic decisions are rarely disclosed in detail. This lack of transparency has led to growing concerns about bias, fairness, and accountability. Policymakers and researchers have called for greater algorithmic transparency, arguing that users should have a better understanding of how their feeds are curated and what data is being used to shape their online experiences.

As social media continues to evolve, algorithms will play an increasingly important role in shaping digital interactions. While they offer undeniable benefits in terms of personalization and content discovery, they also pose significant challenges related to misinformation, privacy, and ethical considerations. Understanding how these algorithms work and their impact on society is essential for navigating the modern digital landscape. The rise of social media algorithms marks a fundamental shift in the way people consume information, interact with content, and engage with the world around them, making it one of the most influential technological developments of the digital age.

Understanding Algorithmic Personalization

Algorithmic personalization has become one of the most influential forces shaping the way people consume content on social media. Every time a user opens an app, whether it is Facebook, Instagram, TikTok, or YouTube, they are met with a feed carefully curated by algorithms designed to predict what will capture their attention. This process is not random. It is the result of a sophisticated system that analyzes user behavior, interests, and engagement history to determine what content should be prioritized. The goal of algorithmic personalization is to create an experience tailored to the preferences of each individual user, keeping them engaged for as long as possible while ensuring they find the platform valuable and entertaining.

The foundation of personalization lies in data collection. Every action taken on a social media platform generates data points that are recorded and analyzed. This includes obvious interactions such as likes, comments, and shares, but it also extends to more subtle behaviors like how long a user lingers on a post, whether they scroll past a video or watch it until the end, and even the speed at which they move through their feed. These signals help platforms build a detailed profile of each user, allowing them to make increasingly accurate predictions about what type of content will hold their interest.

The algorithms responsible for personalization rely heavily on machine learning models that continuously adapt based on user behavior. These models do not just operate at the individual level but also analyze broader trends among users with similar interests. If a group of people who frequently engage with the same kind of content suddenly starts interacting with a new trend, the algorithm takes note and begins recommending that trend to other users who share similar behaviors.

This ability to detect patterns on a large scale enables platforms to keep content fresh and engaging while ensuring that users remain active for extended periods.

Personalization extends beyond social media feeds. It plays a crucial role in recommendation systems across platforms like YouTube, Netflix, and Spotify, where algorithms suggest videos, movies, or songs based on past consumption patterns. These recommendations are designed to keep users engaged by offering content that aligns with their tastes while also introducing new material that is likely to be well-received. This process is known as collaborative filtering, where the algorithm compares a user's behavior to that of others with similar interests to make highly targeted recommendations.

One of the biggest advantages of algorithmic personalization is its ability to enhance user experience by filtering out irrelevant content and prioritizing what is most engaging. Without it, users would be overwhelmed by the sheer volume of content available, making it difficult to find posts, videos, or articles that align with their interests. By narrowing the focus to what is most relevant, personalization creates a more seamless and enjoyable browsing experience, increasing the likelihood that users will return to the platform repeatedly.

Despite its benefits, algorithmic personalization is not without controversy. One of the most significant concerns is the creation of filter bubbles, where users are consistently exposed to content that reinforces their existing beliefs and interests while excluding opposing viewpoints. This phenomenon can lead to ideological echo chambers, where people only see perspectives that align with their worldview, reducing exposure to diverse opinions and limiting critical thinking. The impact of this effect is particularly evident in political and social discussions, where algorithmic curation can contribute to polarization by amplifying extreme or emotionally charged content that drives engagement.

Another major concern is the potential for manipulation. Because social media algorithms prioritize content based on engagement, they often promote posts that trigger strong emotional reactions, whether positive or negative. This can lead to the spread of sensationalized or misleading information, as content that provokes outrage or excitement is more likely to be widely shared. Misinformation thrives in an environment where algorithms reward engagement above accuracy, making it difficult for users to distinguish between credible sources and misleading narratives. This issue has raised ethical questions about the responsibility of social media companies in moderating content and ensuring that their platforms do not contribute to the spread of false information.

Privacy is another key issue tied to algorithmic personalization. In order to create highly customized experiences, platforms collect vast amounts of user data, often without users fully understanding how their information is being used. The collection of personal data raises concerns about surveillance, data security, and the potential for misuse. High-profile scandals, such as the Cambridge Analytica incident, have highlighted the risks associated with data-driven personalization, leading to increased scrutiny from regulators and growing calls for stricter privacy protections. While some platforms have introduced transparency measures, such as giving users more control over their data and personalization settings, many users remain unaware of the extent to which their information is being used to shape their online experience.

Algorithmic personalization also affects content creators and businesses, who must navigate constantly changing ranking systems to maintain visibility. Since engagement metrics dictate which posts are seen by the most people, creators are incentivized to optimize their content for the algorithm, often leading to a homogenization of styles and formats. The pressure to produce content that aligns with algorithmic trends can stifle creativity and originality, as creators prioritize strategies that maximize reach over artistic or informational value. Small businesses and independent creators may struggle to gain traction if their content does not fit within the parameters favored by the algorithm, making it harder to compete with established influencers and brands that have already mastered the system.

As social media platforms continue to refine their personalization algorithms, the balance between user experience, engagement, and ethical considerations remains a topic of ongoing debate. While personalization makes content consumption more efficient and enjoyable, it also raises significant concerns about privacy, misinformation, and the narrowing of perspectives. Understanding how these algorithms function is crucial for both users and policymakers seeking to create a more transparent and equitable digital environment. The more people become aware of the mechanisms driving their online experiences, the better equipped they will be to navigate social media responsibly and critically evaluate the content they consume.

The Role of Machine Learning in Social Media

Machine learning has become the backbone of modern social media platforms, shaping the way users interact with content, discover new trends, and engage with online communities. Every action taken on social media, from liking a post to watching a video, feeds into sophisticated machine learning models that continuously refine and optimize the user experience. These algorithms do not operate in isolation; they are designed to learn from vast amounts of data, identifying patterns and predicting user behavior with remarkable accuracy. By leveraging machine learning, social media platforms can offer highly personalized feeds, recommend relevant content, detect harmful activities, and even enhance user interactions in ways that were unimaginable just a few years ago.

One of the most fundamental roles of machine learning in social media is content curation. Platforms like Facebook, Instagram, and TikTok rely on complex algorithms to determine what appears on a user's feed. Rather than presenting content in chronological order, machine learning models analyze past interactions, engagement history, and behavioral patterns to predict which posts are most likely to capture a user's attention. These models take into account factors such as how long a user watches a video, the types of posts they engage with, and even subtle cues like the speed at which they scroll through content. The more data the system collects, the better it becomes at tailoring content to individual preferences, creating an addictive and highly personalized experience.

Recommendation systems powered by machine learning have also transformed how users discover content. YouTube, for example, uses deep learning models to analyze watch history and suggest videos that align with a user's interests. These recommendations are based on collaborative filtering, where the system identifies patterns among users with similar viewing habits and suggests content that others in the same category have enjoyed. The same principle applies to platforms like Spotify and Netflix, where machine learning helps users find music, movies, and TV shows that match their tastes. The effectiveness of these recommendation systems has made them a crucial part of user engagement strategies, keeping audiences engaged for extended periods and driving increased platform usage.

Machine learning also plays a critical role in content moderation, helping platforms detect and remove harmful or inappropriate content at scale. With billions of posts, comments, and messages shared daily, it is impossible for human moderators to review everything manually. Machine learning models are trained to recognize patterns associated with hate speech, misinformation, and harmful behavior, allowing for automated detection and enforcement. Natural language processing (NLP) techniques enable these models to understand context, tone, and sentiment, making them more effective at identifying problematic content. While no system is perfect, advancements in machine learning have significantly improved the ability of social media platforms to create safer digital environments.

In addition to content moderation, machine learning is instrumental in detecting fake accounts, spam, and bot activity. Platforms like Twitter and Facebook deploy algorithms to identify suspicious behavior, such as rapid posting, coordinated engagement patterns, and unnatural interactions. These systems use anomaly detection techniques to flag accounts that exhibit characteristics commonly associated with bots or malicious actors. By automatically detecting and removing such accounts, machine learning helps maintain the integrity of online conversations and prevents the spread of disinformation. The ongoing battle against spam and fake news is an arms race between social media companies and bad actors who constantly evolve their tactics to bypass detection mechanisms.

Another crucial application of machine learning in social media is sentiment analysis, which helps platforms gauge public opinion and user reactions. Companies use sentiment analysis to track how people feel about specific topics, products, or events by analyzing the language and tone of posts, comments, and reviews. This data is invaluable for businesses, marketers, and policymakers who want to understand consumer sentiment and societal trends. Social media platforms themselves use sentiment analysis to improve user experience, detecting when users express frustration or dissatisfaction and adjusting recommendations accordingly. This technology also enables brands to engage with their audiences more effectively, responding to feedback in real-time and adapting their messaging based on audience sentiment.

Advertising is another domain where machine learning plays a central role in social media. Platforms generate revenue by serving targeted ads, and machine learning algorithms optimize ad delivery by predicting which advertisements are most likely to resonate with individual users. These models analyze user demographics, interests, browsing behavior, and engagement history to match ads with the right audience. By continuously learning from user interactions, the system refines its targeting capabilities, ensuring that advertisers achieve higher conversion rates while users see ads that align with their preferences. This hyper-personalized approach to advertising has made social media an incredibly lucrative space for marketers, but it has also raised concerns about privacy and data exploitation.

Machine learning has also revolutionized the way social media platforms handle image and video recognition. Advanced computer vision techniques allow algorithms to analyze visual content, identifying objects, faces, and even emotions within images and videos. This capability is particularly useful for content moderation, as it enables platforms to detect explicit or inappropriate material without relying solely on user reports. Facial recognition technology, while controversial, is also being integrated into social media experiences, allowing users to tag friends in photos automatically or unlock personalized features based on their facial expressions. However, the use of such technology has sparked debates about privacy, surveillance, and ethical considerations, leading to increased regulatory scrutiny.

The role of machine learning in social media extends beyond just content curation, moderation, and advertising. It is also shaping new forms of interaction and engagement. AI-driven chatbots are being used by brands and businesses to provide customer support, answer inquiries, and even facilitate transactions directly within social media platforms. Virtual influencers—AI-generated characters with realistic appearances and personalities—are gaining popularity, blurring the line between human and machine-generated content. Augmented reality (AR) filters, commonly used on Snapchat and Instagram, are another example of how machine learning enhances user experiences, enabling real-time facial tracking and interactive effects.

As social media platforms continue to evolve, machine learning will become even more deeply embedded in their ecosystems. The ability to process vast amounts of data, identify patterns, and predict user behavior has made machine learning an indispensable tool for optimizing engagement, improving safety, and driving business growth. While these advancements have created highly personalized and efficient digital experiences, they have also introduced ethical dilemmas regarding privacy, algorithmic bias, and the potential for manipulation. The increasing reliance on machine learning in social media raises important questions about transparency, accountability, and the long-term impact of algorithm-driven interactions on human behavior and society as a whole.

How Social Media Platforms Rank Content

Social media platforms operate on vast amounts of content being uploaded every second, making it impossible for users to see everything posted by the people, pages, and brands they follow. To manage this overwhelming volume of information, platforms use ranking algorithms that determine which content appears in a user's feed, in what order, and how frequently. These ranking systems are designed to keep users engaged by showing them content that is most likely to capture their attention based on their past behaviors, preferences, and interactions. The criteria used to rank content vary from platform to platform, but all social media sites share the fundamental goal of maximizing engagement while maintaining a positive user experience.

At the core of content ranking is the concept of relevance. Platforms analyze each piece of content based on numerous factors to determine how relevant it is to individual users. One of the most important factors is engagement. Posts that receive high levels of interaction, such as likes, shares, comments, and watch time, are more likely to be ranked higher in a user's feed. The assumption behind this ranking strategy is that if a post generates significant engagement from other users, it is likely to be interesting or valuable to a broader audience. Engagement signals also include indirect behaviors, such as how long a user spends looking at a post before scrolling past it, whether they pause to read a caption, or if they click on a link or profile after viewing a post.

Another major factor in content ranking is recency. While social media feeds are no longer strictly chronological, the freshness of a post still plays a role in determining its visibility. Most platforms prioritize recent content to ensure that users are seeing up-to-date and relevant posts. However, recency alone is not enough to guarantee high rankings. Even the newest content must meet engagement and quality criteria to be prominently displayed. Older content can sometimes be resurfaced if it continues to receive engagement over time, especially on platforms like YouTube and TikTok, where videos can go viral weeks or even months after being uploaded.

Personalization also plays a crucial role in ranking content. Social media platforms track individual user behaviors and use machine learning models to predict what kind of content each person is most likely to engage with. If a user frequently interacts with posts about fitness, for example, the algorithm will prioritize fitness-related content in their feed. This personalization extends beyond just the topics of interest. The algorithm also considers the types of content formats a user prefers, such as videos, images, or text-based posts. A user who watches long-form videos will be shown more of that type of content, while someone who primarily engages with short clips or memes will see more of those.

The relationships between users also influence content ranking. Platforms prioritize showing posts from close connections, such as friends, family members, and frequently interacted-with accounts. Facebook, for instance, adjusted its algorithm to favor content from friends and family over posts from businesses or media pages, under the assumption that personal connections drive more meaningful engagement. Instagram and Twitter also use relationship strength as a ranking factor, displaying posts from accounts a user frequently engages with before showing content from less-interacted-with sources. This relationship-based ranking ensures that users see posts from people they care about, reinforcing their social connections within the platform.

Content quality is another important aspect of ranking. Platforms use various signals to determine whether a post is high-quality, informative, or entertaining. This assessment is particularly relevant for news articles, videos, and educational content. Facebook, for example, evaluates the credibility of news sources and reduces the visibility of clickbait or misleading headlines. YouTube ranks videos based on factors like production quality, watch time, and viewer retention. TikTok assesses the quality of videos based on how many people watch them all the way through and whether they are shared widely. The goal of ranking high-quality content is to ensure that users receive valuable and engaging material rather than being bombarded with low-effort or misleading posts.

Another factor influencing content ranking is platform-specific priorities. Social media companies often adjust their algorithms to promote certain types of content that align with their strategic goals. For example, Instagram has placed a growing emphasis on video content, particularly Reels, as it competes with TikTok. As a result, videos are given preferential treatment in users' feeds compared to static images. Similarly, Twitter prioritizes trending topics and real-time conversations, pushing tweets related to current events to the top of users' feeds. These platform-driven changes can significantly impact how content is ranked and what types of posts gain the most visibility.

External influences, such as advertisers and sponsored content, also affect ranking. Social media platforms rely on advertising revenue, and paid promotions are integrated into feeds alongside organic content. While advertisements are marked as sponsored, they are still ranked based on engagement and relevance criteria similar to organic posts.

Advertisers use sophisticated targeting tools to ensure their content reaches users most likely to be interested in their products or services. This means that, in addition to organic ranking factors, users often see ads tailored to their behaviors, location, and demographics. Sponsored content competes for user attention alongside regular posts, making the ranking landscape even more complex.

Platform-wide algorithm updates can significantly shift content ranking dynamics. Social media companies frequently tweak their algorithms to refine user experience, combat spam, and adjust to changing trends. These updates can have major implications for content creators and businesses, who must constantly adapt their strategies to maintain visibility. Some algorithm changes are intended to reduce the spread of misinformation, while others aim to balance engagement with user well-being by limiting excessive screen time or reducing the visibility of potentially harmful content. Because these changes are rarely fully disclosed to the public, content creators and marketers must experiment and analyze engagement data to understand how ranking shifts affect their reach.

The process of ranking content on social media is both dynamic and complex, shaped by a combination of engagement, personalization, relationships, content quality, platform priorities, and external influences. While these algorithms are designed to enhance user experience and keep people engaged, they also raise important questions about transparency, fairness, and the ethical implications of automated content curation. The ranking mechanisms that determine what appears in a user's feed have the power to shape public discourse, influence opinions, and dictate which voices are amplified or suppressed. Understanding how social media platforms rank content is essential for both users and content creators who wish to navigate these digital spaces effectively.

The Evolution of Engagement-Based Algorithms

Engagement-based algorithms have fundamentally reshaped the way content is distributed and consumed on social media. In the early days of digital platforms, feeds were primarily chronological, displaying posts in the order they were published. This system was simple and predictable, but as social media networks grew and the volume of content increased exponentially, platforms needed a more efficient way to prioritize what users saw. The solution came in the form of engagement-based algorithms, which transformed social media from a passive experience into a highly personalized and interactive digital environment. These algorithms have since evolved to become the driving force behind what content gets amplified, which creators gain visibility, and how users interact with information online.

The transition from chronological feeds to engagement-driven ranking systems was not just about improving user experience but also about increasing platform retention. Social media companies realized that users were more likely to spend time on their platforms if they saw content that was interesting and relevant to them. By analyzing user interactions such as likes, shares, comments, and time spent on posts, platforms began prioritizing content that generated the most engagement. The assumption behind this strategy was that content receiving high levels of interaction was inherently more valuable, and therefore, should be pushed to more users.

Facebook was one of the first major platforms to adopt an engagement-based approach, introducing the EdgeRank algorithm, which determined the likelihood of a post appearing in a user's feed based on factors such as affinity, weight, and decay. Affinity measured the relationship between the user and the content creator, weight assigned value to different types of engagement, and decay ensured that older posts would gradually lose visibility over time. This early model laid the foundation for more sophisticated ranking mechanisms that would soon be adopted across the industry.

As engagement algorithms became more advanced, they started incorporating deeper behavioral analysis. Rather than relying solely on direct interactions, platforms began tracking passive engagement signals, such as how long users hovered over a post, whether they clicked on embedded links, and even how quickly they scrolled through their feeds. Machine learning models were trained to predict user preferences with increasing accuracy, refining the ranking of posts based on complex behavioral patterns. This shift made engagement algorithms more effective at curating content but also made them more opaque, as users had little insight into why certain posts appeared more frequently than others.

One of the most significant turning points in the evolution of engagement algorithms was the rise of video content. Platforms quickly recognized that videos drove higher engagement rates than static images or text-based posts. Facebook and Instagram adjusted their algorithms to prioritize video content, leading to the widespread adoption of video posts among content creators and brands. YouTube, which had always been video-focused, introduced watch time as a key ranking factor, replacing view count as the primary metric for determining video relevance. This change encouraged creators to produce longer, more engaging videos rather than focusing solely on attracting clicks. TikTok took engagement-based ranking to a new level by using a fully algorithmic feed on its For You Page, where videos were surfaced based purely on user behavior rather than social connections. This approach allowed content to go viral organically, even if it was posted by an unknown creator with a small following.

The dominance of engagement-driven algorithms also led to unintended consequences, particularly in the spread of sensational and polarizing content. Studies have shown that emotionally charged posts—whether they evoke outrage, joy, or fear—tend to receive higher engagement, leading platforms to prioritize such content. This dynamic contributed to the rapid spread of misinformation, conspiracy theories, and divisive political rhetoric, as posts that generated strong reactions were systematically boosted by the algorithm. The phenomenon of engagement-driven amplification raised ethical concerns about the role of social media in shaping public discourse and influencing opinions.

To counteract some of these negative effects, platforms began introducing additional signals to their ranking systems. Facebook adjusted its algorithm to prioritize meaningful interactions, placing greater emphasis on content from close friends and family rather than viral posts from pages and public figures. Instagram and Twitter incorporated signals aimed at reducing the reach of low-quality or misleading content, implementing fact-checking initiatives and content warnings for flagged posts. YouTube took steps to limit the visibility of conspiracy-driven content by adjusting its recommendation algorithm to prioritize authoritative sources.

Despite these efforts, engagement-based algorithms remain highly susceptible to manipulation. Clickbait tactics, engagement baiting, and coordinated inauthentic behavior are commonly used to game the system. Content creators and marketers have adapted their strategies to align with algorithmic preferences, often tailoring their posts to maximize engagement at the expense of quality or originality. This has led to a homogenization of content, where posts follow predictable formats designed to trigger interactions rather than provide value.

The growing reliance on engagement-based ranking has also created challenges for small creators and businesses trying to gain visibility. As algorithms prioritize content from accounts that already receive high engagement, new or less-established creators may struggle to break through. To address this, some platforms have introduced features designed to give emerging voices a chance, such as TikTok's ability to surface content from small accounts based on its immediate engagement performance rather than historical popularity.

Another area of evolution in engagement algorithms is the integration of artificial intelligence to refine personalization. Platforms now use deep learning models to analyze not only individual user behavior but also broader engagement trends across different demographics and geographic regions. This level of data-driven optimization allows platforms to adjust ranking systems in real-time, responding to shifting user interests and external events. Social media companies also experiment with new ranking factors, such as prioritizing posts that encourage longer conversations or that align with platform-wide initiatives, such as sustainability or mental health awareness.

As engagement-based algorithms continue to evolve, they will likely become even more sophisticated, incorporating multimodal analysis that considers text, image, video, and audio data simultaneously. The future of content ranking may involve a hybrid approach that balances engagement with other factors, such as credibility, context, and ethical considerations. Social media platforms face an ongoing challenge in fine-tuning their algorithms to maintain user engagement while mitigating harmful effects such as misinformation, polarization, and addiction. The continued refinement of engagement-based ranking systems will shape the way digital interactions unfold, influencing not only entertainment and communication but also the broader societal landscape in ways that are still unfolding.

The Power of Likes, Shares, and Comments

Social media platforms thrive on interaction. Every post, video, or comment exists within an ecosystem fueled by engagement, and at the heart of this system are likes, shares, and comments. These simple actions have evolved from basic user interactions into powerful tools that dictate visibility, influence, and even the emotional experiences of individuals online. What started as a way for users to express appreciation or agreement has transformed into a mechanism that shapes digital conversations, determines content reach, and influences societal trends. The power of engagement metrics extends beyond personal interactions, impacting businesses, politics, and the very way people perceive reality in the digital age.

Likes are the most fundamental form of engagement on social media. They provide instant feedback, signaling approval or support with the tap of a finger. The psychological impact of receiving likes is well-documented, with studies showing that each notification triggers a release of dopamine, reinforcing behavior and encouraging users to continue posting. This positive reinforcement loop keeps people engaged on platforms, seeking validation and interaction from their peers. The number of likes a post receives also serves as a social proof mechanism, influencing how others perceive its value. Content with a high number of likes is often seen as more credible, appealing, or popular, creating a bandwagon effect where users are more likely to engage with a post simply because it has already garnered attention.

Shares hold even greater power in determining the reach of content. Unlike likes, which only provide a personal endorsement, sharing actively distributes content to new audiences. When a user shares a post, it extends beyond its original network, gaining visibility in new circles and increasing the potential for virality. Social media algorithms prioritize shared content because it signals high relevance and resonance. A post that receives a significant number of shares is likely to appear in more users' feeds, sometimes even being pushed to trending sections or recommended lists. This amplification effect makes shares one of the most valuable engagement metrics, particularly for content creators, businesses, and influencers seeking to expand their reach.

The virality of certain posts often begins with a chain reaction of shares. A single tweet, meme, or video can be shared millions of times, spreading across platforms and reaching global audiences in a matter of hours. This phenomenon has given rise to digital trends, memes, and challenges that shape internet culture. However, the same mechanisms that make content go viral can also contribute to the rapid spread of misinformation. False or misleading content often gains traction because it elicits strong emotional reactions, prompting users to share it before verifying its accuracy. The ease with which information spreads through shares has raised concerns about the role of social media in the dissemination of fake news, propaganda, and conspiracy theories.

Comments add another layer of complexity to engagement dynamics. Unlike likes and shares, which are relatively passive, comments require direct participation and foster conversations. The comment section of a post serves as a digital forum where users express opinions, debate topics, and engage in discussions. Comments can significantly influence the perception of a post, as users often read them before forming their own opinions. A post with overwhelmingly positive comments can reinforce its credibility, while a flood of negative comments can cast doubt on its validity. This social validation process impacts how users interpret content and contributes to the formation of collective opinions.

The presence of comments also plays a crucial role in algorithmic ranking. Posts that generate a high number of comments are often given priority in feeds because they signal deep engagement. Algorithms favor discussions, assuming that if people are taking the time to comment, the content is provoking meaningful interaction. This has led content creators to actively encourage comments by posing questions, sparking debates, or using engagement bait techniques such as "Comment your favorite emoji if you agree!" While these strategies can boost visibility, they have also contributed to the gamification of social media, where content is optimized for engagement rather than authenticity or quality.

The influence of likes, shares, and comments extends beyond individual posts, shaping user behavior and content creation strategies. Social media personalities, brands, and influencers rely on engagement metrics to measure success and refine their approach. High engagement rates translate into increased visibility, sponsorship opportunities, and financial incentives. Many platforms have introduced monetization features that reward creators based on engagement, further reinforcing the importance of likes, shares, and comments as currency in the digital world. This emphasis on engagement has led to an industry of social media optimization, where businesses and influencers meticulously craft content designed to maximize interaction.

The pursuit of engagement has also given rise to ethical concerns. The desire for likes and shares can drive users to post sensationalized, exaggerated, or even harmful content in an effort to attract attention. Clickbait headlines, misleading thumbnails, and controversial statements are often used as tactics to generate reactions, regardless of accuracy or ethical considerations. Social media platforms have struggled to balance engagement-driven algorithms with responsible content curation, implementing measures such as fact-checking labels, content moderation, and demotion of engagement bait. However, these efforts are often met with resistance, as platforms also rely on high engagement to drive ad revenue and user retention.

The psychological impact of engagement metrics has also been a subject of debate. The constant pressure to receive likes and positive interactions can lead to anxiety, self-esteem issues, and unhealthy social comparisons. Studies have shown that users who do not receive expected engagement on their posts may experience feelings of rejection or inadequacy. In response to these concerns, some platforms have experimented with hiding like counts, allowing users to focus on content rather than validation. While these changes have been praised for reducing social pressure, engagement remains the driving force behind content visibility and digital influence.

The power of likes, shares, and comments is undeniable, shaping not only individual experiences but also broader social trends and online discourse. They determine which voices are amplified, which messages gain traction, and how information spreads in the digital age. While engagement metrics have democratized content creation, allowing anyone with a smartphone to reach global audiences, they have also introduced challenges related to misinformation, ethical content production, and mental health. As social media continues to evolve, the role of engagement will remain a critical factor in defining the landscape of digital interaction, influencing the way people communicate, consume information, and navigate the complexities of the online world.

The Filter Bubble Effect

The filter bubble effect is one of the most significant consequences of modern social media algorithms, shaping the way individuals consume information and interact with the digital world. As platforms prioritize personalized content to maximize engagement, users are increasingly exposed to a narrow set of viewpoints, interests, and opinions that align with their past behaviors. This creates a self-reinforcing cycle where people encounter content that confirms their existing beliefs while filtering out alternative perspectives. The term filter bubble was popularized by Eli Pariser, who warned that personalized algorithms could lead to intellectual isolation, limiting exposure to diverse viewpoints and reducing the ability to engage with a broader spectrum of ideas.

The rise of personalized algorithms began with the shift away from chronological feeds, as social media platforms sought to improve user experience by showing the most relevant content first. Instead of displaying posts in the order they were published, algorithms now analyze engagement patterns, past interactions, and behavioral data to curate an individualized feed. This level of personalization ensures that users see content they are most likely to engage with, but it also means they are less likely to come across opposing viewpoints or new ideas outside their established interests. The more a user interacts with a certain type of content, the more the algorithm reinforces that preference, creating a digital echo chamber where only similar perspectives are amplified.

One of the key drivers of the filter bubble effect is engagement-based ranking. Social media algorithms are designed to maximize user attention, and they achieve this by prioritizing content that triggers strong emotional responses. Studies have shown that people are more likely to engage with posts that evoke strong feelings, whether it be excitement, outrage, or validation. This has led to a situation where users are repeatedly exposed to content that aligns with their emotional and ideological biases, reinforcing their worldview while minimizing dissenting opinions. Over time, this creates an environment where individuals become more certain of their beliefs, often without realizing that they are only seeing a curated subset of the available information.

The filter bubble effect is particularly evident in political discourse, where social media platforms play a significant role in shaping public opinion. During election cycles or major political events, algorithms prioritize content that aligns with a user's previous interactions, leading to a highly polarized online experience. If a user frequently engages with content that supports a particular political party or ideology, they will see more posts that reinforce those views while being shielded from counterarguments or opposing perspectives. This phenomenon contributes to political polarization, making it harder for individuals to understand or empathize with those who hold different beliefs. In extreme cases, filter bubbles can create entirely separate realities, where people consuming different types of content come to vastly different conclusions about the same events.

The impact of filter bubbles extends beyond politics and into other areas such as science, health, and cultural discourse. During the COVID-19 pandemic, for example, social media platforms became a primary source of information for many people. However, the filter bubble effect meant that some users were primarily exposed to accurate scientific information, while others were inundated with misinformation and conspiracy theories. This divergence in information access influenced public perceptions of the pandemic, vaccine hesitancy, and compliance with health measures. The same dynamic applies to topics such as climate change, where users who frequently engage with scientific discussions are shown more evidence-based content, while those who interact with skepticism or denialist views are more likely to encounter misinformation reinforcing those beliefs.

The filter bubble effect is further intensified by recommendation algorithms, which extend beyond social media feeds to influence video content, search results, and news consumption. Platforms like YouTube use watch history and engagement patterns to suggest videos that align with a user's interests, often leading viewers down a path of increasingly extreme or niche content. This can create a rabbit-hole effect, where users are gradually exposed to more radicalized or conspiratorial views through a series of algorithmically suggested videos. Search engines also contribute to filter bubbles by personalizing results based on past searches and location, subtly shaping the information that users encounter when researching a topic.

Despite the growing awareness of filter bubbles, they are difficult to escape because they are built into the design of social media platforms. Users often do not realize that the content they see is being curated by an algorithm, assuming that their feed reflects a balanced representation of available information. This invisibility makes filter bubbles particularly insidious, as people are unaware of the information they are missing. Even when platforms introduce tools to provide alternative viewpoints, such as fact-checking labels or diverse news recommendations, users often resist engaging with content that contradicts their established beliefs. Psychological factors such as confirmation bias further reinforce the filter bubble effect, as people naturally gravitate toward information that validates their existing opinions.

The consequences of filter bubbles are far-reaching, affecting not only individual understanding but also broader societal cohesion. When people are only exposed to content that aligns with their views, it becomes harder to engage in meaningful discussions with those who think differently. This leads to greater ideological division, reducing the ability to find common ground on important social and political issues. Filter bubbles also affect democratic processes, as voters who only consume one-sided information may struggle to make informed decisions. Additionally, the reinforcement of specific narratives can contribute to misinformation, radicalization, and distrust in institutions, further eroding social cohesion.

Efforts to address the filter bubble effect have been met with mixed success. Some platforms have introduced features that allow users to explore different perspectives, such as Twitter's efforts to display tweets from opposing viewpoints or Facebook's initiatives to promote diverse news sources. However, these changes often conflict with the engagement-driven business model of social media, which benefits from keeping users immersed in familiar and emotionally engaging content. Some researchers and technologists have proposed algorithmic transparency as a solution, advocating for greater user control over how content is ranked and displayed. Others argue for media literacy education to help users recognize and critically evaluate the information they consume online.

The filter bubble effect remains one of the most pressing challenges in the digital age, shaping how people perceive the world and engage with information. While algorithmic personalization has made social media more engaging and efficient, it has also contributed to ideological isolation and information distortion. As technology continues to evolve, finding ways to balance personalization with exposure to diverse perspectives will be crucial in fostering a more informed and connected society. Understanding the mechanics of filter bubbles is the first step toward mitigating their influence, empowering users to take a more active role in curating their own digital experiences and seeking out a broader range of viewpoints.

How Algorithms Shape Public Opinion

Social media algorithms have become one of the most influential forces shaping public opinion in the digital age. These algorithms determine what content users see, how often they see it, and how long it stays in their feeds. By curating information based on past interactions, engagement metrics, and predictive analytics, algorithms create a customized digital environment that significantly impacts what people believe, how they interpret current events, and which narratives gain traction in society. While social media platforms were initially designed to facilitate communication and community-building, their algorithm-driven content distribution systems now play a central role in shaping political discourse, social movements, and even cultural norms.

One of the most significant ways algorithms influence public opinion is through the amplification of certain types of content. Social media platforms prioritize engagement, meaning that posts that receive high levels of likes, shares, and comments are more likely to be promoted in users' feeds. This system rewards emotionally charged content, as studies have shown that posts evoking strong emotions—whether outrage, joy, fear, or excitement—tend to generate more interaction. As a result, the algorithmic prioritization of highly engaging content can create a distorted view of reality, where the most sensationalized or polarizing narratives receive the most visibility, regardless of their accuracy.

The ability of algorithms to amplify specific messages has played a major role in modern political campaigns. Politicians and advocacy groups leverage social media's algorithmic structure to target specific demographics with tailored messaging. By analyzing user behavior, platforms allow political organizations to micro-target audiences with highly customized advertisements and content. This level of personalization means that different groups of people receive vastly different political messages, often reinforcing their pre-existing beliefs and deepening ideological divisions. The use of algorithm-driven advertising has raised concerns about manipulation, as it allows political actors to spread tailored narratives without broader public scrutiny.

Misinformation thrives in an algorithmic environment that prioritizes engagement over accuracy. False or misleading information often spreads faster than factual reporting because it is designed to provoke strong reactions. Conspiracy theories, fake news, and misleading headlines generate outrage and curiosity, making them highly shareable. Once misinformation gains traction, the algorithm further amplifies it, exposing even more users to the misleading narrative. This cycle has contributed to the erosion of trust in traditional news sources, as users increasingly rely on social media for their information. While platforms have introduced fact-checking initiatives and content moderation efforts, misinformation continues to spread rapidly due to the nature of engagement-driven algorithms.

The role of algorithms in shaping public opinion extends beyond politics and misinformation to broader social and cultural issues. Social media platforms have become the primary space for discussions on social justice, activism, and societal change. Movements such as #MeToo, Black Lives Matter, and climate activism have gained widespread visibility largely due to the way algorithms amplify viral content. Hashtags, trending topics, and user-generated content allow social movements to spread messages quickly and mobilize support. However, the same algorithmic mechanisms that amplify activism can also be used to spread divisive or extremist ideologies, demonstrating the dual-edged nature of algorithmic influence.

Echo chambers and filter bubbles further intensify the impact of algorithms on public opinion. By continuously showing users content that aligns with their past interactions and preferences, social media platforms create a self-reinforcing loop where individuals are primarily exposed to information that confirms their existing beliefs. This isolation from opposing viewpoints can lead to increased polarization, as users become more entrenched in their ideological positions. The reinforcement of biases through algorithmic curation makes it difficult for individuals to critically evaluate new information or consider alternative perspectives.

The global nature of social media algorithms means that public opinion is not just shaped at the individual level but also at a societal scale. In times of crisis, such as natural disasters, political uprisings, or global pandemics, social media becomes a key source of information. The way algorithms prioritize and distribute information during these events can have real-world consequences. For example, during public health emergencies, the visibility of scientific information versus misinformation can impact public behavior, trust in institutions, and compliance with safety measures. Similarly, in times of political unrest, algorithmic amplification of certain narratives can escalate tensions, influence protests, and even affect election outcomes.

Corporations and media outlets have also adapted their strategies to align with algorithmic trends. Traditional journalism has been forced to compete with digital-native content that is optimized for social media engagement. This shift has led many news organizations to adjust their headlines, reporting styles, and content formats to fit algorithmic preferences. Clickbait headlines, emotionally charged reporting, and viral-focused storytelling have become more common as media outlets seek to maintain visibility in an environment where engagement determines reach. The economic pressure to produce highly engaging content has contributed to the blurring of lines between news, entertainment, and opinion.

The influence of social media algorithms is not just limited to what information is amplified but also what is suppressed. Algorithmic content moderation plays a role in determining which voices are heard and which are silenced. While platforms remove harmful content such as hate speech and violent extremism, they also make subjective decisions about what constitutes misinformation or harmful discourse. These decisions can be influenced by external factors, including government pressure, corporate interests, and public relations concerns. As a result, there are ongoing debates about censorship, free speech, and the role of private technology companies in regulating public discourse.

As social media continues to evolve, so too will the mechanisms that shape public opinion. Algorithmic influence will likely become even more sophisticated, incorporating artificial intelligence, deep learning, and real-time behavioral analysis to further refine content curation. The introduction of emerging technologies such as augmented reality, virtual influencers, and AI-generated content will add new dimensions to how information is presented and consumed. While these advancements have the potential to enhance digital experiences, they also raise ethical questions about the balance between personalization, transparency, and the integrity of public discourse.

Understanding how algorithms shape public opinion is crucial for navigating the complexities of the digital information landscape. While algorithm-driven content distribution has made information more accessible and personalized, it has also introduced challenges related to misinformation, polarization, and manipulation. The influence of these systems extends beyond social media, impacting journalism, politics, activism, and societal norms. As platforms continue to refine their algorithms, the need for greater transparency, media literacy, and critical thinking skills becomes increasingly important in ensuring that public opinion is shaped by informed discourse rather than algorithmic bias.

The Spread of Misinformation and Fake News

Social media has revolutionized the way people consume information, making it easier than ever to access news, opinions, and real-time updates from around the world. However, this unprecedented level of connectivity has also given rise to a major challenge: the rapid spread of misinformation and fake news. The very algorithms that power social media platforms, designed to maximize engagement and keep users on the platform longer, have inadvertently created an environment where false or misleading information can spread faster than ever before. Unlike traditional news media, which is subject to editorial oversight and journalistic standards, social media allows anyone to publish and share content instantly, often without verification. As a result, misinformation has become a persistent issue that influences public perception, shapes political discourse, and impacts real-world decisions.

One of the main reasons misinformation spreads so easily on social media is that false or exaggerated content often generates strong emotional reactions. People are more likely to engage with posts that provoke outrage, fear, or excitement, and social media algorithms prioritize content that receives high levels of engagement. This creates a cycle where sensational or misleading headlines attract clicks and shares, leading to further visibility and even greater spread. Studies have shown that false news stories travel faster and reach more people than true stories, in part because they are designed to be attention-grabbing. The more shocking or controversial a piece of content is, the more likely it is to go viral, regardless of its accuracy.

The role of social media algorithms in amplifying misinformation is particularly evident in political discourse. During major elections, controversial political events, or global crises, misinformation can spread rapidly, influencing public opinion and even shaping electoral outcomes. Political misinformation often takes the form of misleading statistics, out-of-context quotes, or outright fabrications designed to damage opponents or sway undecided voters. Because social media allows for micro-targeting, political misinformation can be tailored to specific audiences, making it even more effective. Users who already hold certain political beliefs are more likely to engage with and share content that aligns with their views, reinforcing their biases and deepening ideological divisions.

Fake news is not limited to politics. It extends into areas such as health, science, and global events, often with serious consequences. The COVID-19 pandemic highlighted the dangers of misinformation, as false claims about the virus, treatments, and vaccines spread widely across social media. Conspiracy theories about the origins of the virus, unproven cures, and vaccine misinformation led to confusion, distrust in medical authorities, and in some cases, harmful behaviors. Platforms attempted to combat the spread of false health information by adding fact-checking labels, removing misleading posts, and promoting authoritative sources. However, these measures were not always effective, as misinformation continued to circulate in private groups, messaging apps, and alternative platforms.

One of the challenges in addressing misinformation is that many users struggle to distinguish between credible sources and unreliable ones. Unlike traditional media, which has established reputations and editorial standards, social media blurs the line between professional journalism and user-generated content. Fake news sites often mimic the appearance of legitimate news outlets, using official-sounding names, professional designs, and fabricated statistics to create the illusion of credibility. The speed at which information spreads also makes it difficult for fact-checkers to keep up, as false claims can reach millions of users before they are debunked. Even when corrections are made, misinformation can be difficult to erase, as people tend to remember the initial claim more than the correction.

Misinformation is also fueled by the way social media encourages echo chambers and filter bubbles. Algorithms prioritize content that aligns with a user's previous interactions, meaning that people are often exposed to information that reinforces their existing beliefs. This makes it easier for false narratives to take hold, as users rarely encounter opposing viewpoints or fact-based corrections. Once misinformation is embedded within an echo chamber, it becomes self-reinforcing, with members of the group sharing and validating the same misleading claims. Over time, these false narratives can become deeply ingrained, making it even harder to correct them with factual information.

Another factor that contributes to the spread of misinformation is the rise of deepfake technology and AI-generated content. Advances in artificial intelligence have made it possible to create highly realistic fake videos, images, and audio recordings that can deceive even trained observers. Deepfake videos of public figures making false statements, for example, can be used to manipulate public opinion and discredit political opponents. AI-generated text can be used to produce fake news articles, blog posts, and social media comments that appear authentic. As these technologies become more sophisticated, distinguishing between real and fake content will become even more challenging, increasing the risk of misinformation on social media.

Social media companies have taken steps to combat misinformation, but their efforts have been met with mixed results. Fact-checking initiatives, content moderation, and algorithmic adjustments have been implemented to reduce the visibility of false information. Some platforms have introduced warning labels on misleading posts, directing users to verified sources. Others have downranked or removed content flagged as false by independent fact-checkers. However, these measures are not always effective, as misinformation often finds new ways to spread. Users who distrust mainstream media may reject fact-checking efforts, viewing them as censorship rather than correction. Additionally, misinformation frequently migrates to private groups, encrypted messaging services, and alternative platforms where moderation is less strict.

Governments and policymakers have also attempted to address misinformation through legislation and regulation. Some countries have introduced laws requiring social media platforms to take stronger action against fake news, while others have imposed penalties for spreading false information. However, regulating online content raises complex questions about free speech, censorship, and the role of private companies in controlling public discourse. Striking a balance between limiting harmful misinformation and preserving open debate remains a major challenge. Efforts to regulate social media must also consider the global nature of misinformation, as content can easily cross borders and influence audiences in different countries.

Media literacy has been proposed as a long-term solution to combat misinformation. Educating users on how to critically evaluate online information, verify sources, and recognize manipulative tactics can help reduce the spread of false content. Schools, universities, and organizations have developed programs to teach digital literacy, encouraging individuals to question the accuracy of the information they encounter online. Some social media platforms have also launched educational campaigns, providing users with tips on how to identify fake news and avoid spreading misinformation. While media literacy initiatives are promising, they require widespread adoption and continuous reinforcement to be effective.

The spread of misinformation and fake news on social media is a complex issue with far-reaching implications. The very algorithms designed to personalize content and enhance engagement have also made it easier for false narratives to spread rapidly, influencing public perception and real-world events. Efforts to combat misinformation must balance platform responsibility, user education, and policy interventions while navigating the challenges of free speech and digital governance. As technology continues to evolve, the fight against misinformation will require constant adaptation, vigilance, and cooperation between social media companies, governments, and the public. Understanding how misinformation spreads and why it thrives on social media is essential to developing effective strategies for addressing it in the future.

Algorithmic Bias: Who Gets Seen and Who Doesn't

Algorithmic bias is one of the most controversial and least understood aspects of social media. While algorithms are designed to personalize content and optimize engagement, they do not operate in a vacuum. They are built using data, trained on patterns, and shaped by human decisions at every stage of their development. As a result, biases—both intentional and unintentional—become embedded in the systems that dictate what content is seen, who gains visibility, and which voices are amplified or suppressed. These biases influence everything from social movements to job opportunities, shaping the way information flows online and determining who has a platform in the digital age.

The core of algorithmic bias lies in the data that fuels machine learning models. Algorithms are not inherently fair or neutral; they reflect the biases present in the data they are trained on. If a dataset is skewed toward a particular demographic, cultural perspective, or behavioral pattern, the algorithm will learn and replicate those biases. This becomes particularly problematic when applied to social media ranking systems, which determine which posts appear at the top of a feed, whose videos go viral, and which creators receive the most exposure. If an algorithm is trained on data that overrepresents certain groups while underrepresenting others, it will disproportionately favor the dominant group while limiting visibility for others.

The impact of algorithmic bias can be seen in how different types of content perform on various platforms. Studies have shown that posts from marginalized communities often receive lower engagement or are deprioritized by ranking systems. This occurs for several reasons, one of which is the historical bias encoded in natural language processing models. AI systems used to moderate and rank content have been found to misinterpret or flag certain dialects, cultural expressions, and topics as inappropriate or less relevant. For example, African American

Vernacular English (AAVE) has been disproportionately flagged as offensive by automated moderation systems, leading to reduced visibility for Black creators. Similarly, discussions of LGBTQ+ issues, feminist perspectives, or content related to social justice have, at times, been downranked or demonetized due to the way algorithms classify sensitive topics.

Facial recognition and image-processing algorithms have also been criticized for biased outcomes. Studies have revealed that facial recognition technology struggles to accurately detect and classify individuals with darker skin tones compared to lighter-skinned individuals. This issue extends into social media, where image-based algorithms influence which photos and videos are promoted. If an algorithm is biased in how it identifies and processes visual content, it may favor certain aesthetics, skin tones, or facial features over others, resulting in an unequal distribution of visibility. This phenomenon has led to accusations that platforms reinforce beauty standards that align with Western ideals, marginalizing users who do not fit into those narrow definitions.

Algorithmic bias is further reinforced by the way engagement-based ranking systems operate. Content that receives early engagement is more likely to be promoted to a wider audience, creating a feedback loop where already-popular creators continue to grow while smaller or less favored voices struggle to gain traction. If a platform's user base or initial engagement trends favor a specific demographic, the algorithm will continue amplifying content from that group while limiting exposure for others. This is particularly evident in influencer culture, where certain creators achieve massive reach while others, despite producing high-quality content, struggle to gain visibility due to algorithmic favoritism.

Advertising algorithms also play a significant role in shaping who gets seen and who doesn't. Social media platforms use machine learning to optimize ad targeting, ensuring that advertisements reach the users most likely to engage with them. However, this process can reinforce existing biases, particularly when it comes to job postings, housing advertisements, and financial opportunities. Investigations have revealed that platforms have, at times, displayed job ads based on gender stereotypes, showing high-paying executive positions to men more often than to women. Similarly, real estate ads have been shown to be delivered along racial and socioeconomic lines, limiting access to certain housing opportunities based on historical patterns of discrimination. These biased ad distribution patterns reflect the ways in which algorithms can perpetuate social inequalities rather than correcting them.

One of the most troubling aspects of algorithmic bias is that it is often invisible to users. People may assume that their feeds represent a neutral or organic selection of content when, in reality, the algorithm has already filtered and ranked what they see. This lack of transparency makes it difficult to identify when bias is occurring or to challenge the systems that reinforce it. Even when social media companies make adjustments to their algorithms in response to bias concerns, the changes are rarely made fully transparent to the public, leaving users uncertain about how their content is being ranked and whether they are being fairly represented.

Efforts to address algorithmic bias have been met with both progress and resistance. Some platforms have introduced diversity audits to analyze how their algorithms affect different demographic groups, while others have implemented bias-detection frameworks to minimize discrimination in their ranking systems. However, these efforts are often reactive rather than proactive, addressing bias only after public outcry or legal pressure. Moreover, because engagement-driven algorithms prioritize profitability and user retention, there is little incentive for companies to fundamentally change systems that have been optimized for maximizing interaction, even if they contribute to biased outcomes.

The presence of algorithmic bias raises deeper questions about fairness, equity, and digital representation. If social media is now the primary space for public discourse, cultural expression, and economic opportunity, then algorithmic bias has real-world consequences. It affects who gets hired, which social movements gain traction, whose businesses succeed, and which ideas shape mainstream conversations. The ability to be seen, heard, and recognized in the digital space is not just about personal validation—it is about access to opportunities, influence, and the ability to participate in global conversations.

As social media platforms continue to evolve, the challenge of algorithmic bias will remain an ongoing concern. While technological solutions such as more inclusive training data, human oversight, and bias-mitigation tools can help, they are not enough on their own. The broader conversation about algorithmic bias must also include discussions about power, accountability, and the ethical responsibility of tech companies to ensure that their platforms do not perpetuate or exacerbate social inequalities. The issue of who gets seen and who doesn't is not just about technology—it is about the values embedded within the systems that govern the digital world and the societal impact they create.

Shadowbanning and Content Moderation

Social media platforms have become the primary spaces for digital communication, public discourse, and content creation. However, as these platforms have grown, they have had to develop systems to manage the vast amount of content being produced every second. Content moderation is one of the most essential and controversial aspects of social media management. It determines what content is allowed, what is removed, and what is quietly suppressed. One of the most debated and least understood practices within content moderation is shadowbanning, a form of suppression where a user's posts or account visibility is reduced without any direct notification. Unlike outright bans, where users are informed that their content has been removed or their account has been suspended, shadowbanning operates in a way that often leaves users unaware that they have been restricted, making it one of the most frustrating and mysterious aspects of platform governance.

Shadowbanning is not an official policy on most platforms, yet many users suspect that it happens regularly. The idea behind shadowbanning is that instead of outright removing content or banning an account, the platform limits the reach of the user's posts, making them invisible or less visible to others. This can happen in several ways, including preventing a user's content from appearing in hashtag searches, excluding posts from algorithmic recommendations, or limiting engagement by making it harder for others to see or interact with their content. The user may still be able to post normally, but their reach is significantly reduced without them knowing why. This lack of transparency leads to confusion, speculation, and frustration, particularly among content creators who rely on engagement for their livelihood.

The origins of shadowbanning can be traced back to early internet forums, where moderators would sometimes silence disruptive users by making their posts visible only to them while remaining hidden from others. This was a way to curb spam and toxic behavior without directly engaging in arguments or fueling further disruption. As social media evolved, similar tactics began appearing on major platforms as a way to handle problematic content, reduce misinformation, or limit content deemed inappropriate by automated moderation systems. Unlike traditional moderation, which involves direct intervention such as content removal or account suspension, shadowbanning works in the background, making it difficult to detect and even harder to appeal.

Content moderation is a necessary function of any social media platform, as it helps remove harmful material such as hate speech, violent content, misinformation, and harassment. However, the way moderation decisions are made, especially when they involve automated systems, has raised concerns about fairness, accuracy, and bias. Platforms use artificial intelligence and machine learning to scan vast amounts of content for violations of community guidelines, but these systems are not perfect. Automated moderation can misinterpret context, flagging content as inappropriate when it is not, or failing to catch genuinely harmful material. Shadowbanning often results from these automated processes, where content is downranked or suppressed due to algorithmic decisions rather than direct human intervention.

One of the biggest issues with shadowbanning is the lack of transparency. Users who experience a sudden drop in engagement, disappearing posts, or unexplained reach limitations often struggle to determine whether they have been shadowbanned or if the algorithm has simply changed. Platforms rarely provide clear explanations or notifications when content is suppressed, leaving users to guess whether their posts have been restricted. This creates an atmosphere of distrust, where users feel that they are being unfairly silenced without understanding why. Content creators, influencers, and businesses that depend on social media for exposure and income are particularly vulnerable to shadowbanning, as even a small reduction in visibility can have significant financial consequences.

Social media companies have denied the existence of shadowbanning in its strictest sense, arguing that any perceived suppression is the result of normal algorithmic adjustments rather than intentional silencing. However, leaked internal documents and former employees have confirmed that platforms do use tactics that resemble shadowbanning, including downranking content that is deemed borderline inappropriate, limiting the visibility of posts that receive user reports, or reducing exposure for accounts that engage in repeated violations of community guidelines. While these practices may be designed to maintain a safer online environment, the lack of transparency around them has led to widespread frustration and conspiracy theories about social media censorship.

The effects of shadowbanning are not evenly distributed across all users. Studies and user reports suggest that marginalized communities, political activists, and certain types of content creators are more likely to be affected by content suppression. Activists who discuss controversial topics, artists who create provocative content, and independent journalists reporting on sensitive issues have all reported experiencing sudden drops in engagement, leading to speculation that their content is being deliberately suppressed. Social media platforms have faced accusations of bias in their moderation decisions, with some groups claiming that their viewpoints are unfairly targeted while others are given preferential treatment.

Content moderation policies vary from platform to platform, with some being stricter than others in enforcing their rules. Facebook and Instagram have faced criticism for their policies around nudity, which often result in the removal or suppression of artwork, body-positive content, and educational material while allowing other, more questionable content to remain. Twitter has been accused of inconsistently enforcing its rules on hate speech and harassment, with some users being permanently suspended while others, despite repeated violations, remain active. TikTok has been particularly criticized for allegedly suppressing content from disabled users,

LGBTQ+ creators, and people of color under the guise of reducing bullying, raising concerns about algorithmic discrimination.

The debate over shadowbanning and content moderation is part of a larger discussion about free speech, platform accountability, and digital governance. While social media companies are private entities with the right to enforce their own rules, they also function as public spaces where millions of people engage in discourse, share ideas, and build communities. The decisions made by content moderation teams and algorithmic ranking systems influence which voices are heard and which are silenced. The challenge lies in balancing the need for moderation with the right to free expression, ensuring that harmful content is controlled without unfairly restricting legitimate speech.

The future of content moderation and shadowbanning will likely involve a combination of improved transparency, better communication between platforms and users, and more refined AI moderation systems. Some platforms have begun experimenting with ways to provide users with clearer explanations when their content is restricted, offering appeal processes and feedback mechanisms to address unfair moderation decisions. Others have proposed decentralized moderation models, where communities have more control over their own content policies rather than relying on top-down enforcement from platform owners.

As social media continues to evolve, the role of moderation in shaping online discourse will remain a critical issue. Shadowbanning, whether intentional or algorithmic, raises important questions about fairness, accountability, and the power of technology companies to control digital speech. While content moderation is necessary to maintain safe and productive online spaces, it must be implemented with transparency, consistency, and fairness to ensure that all users have an equal opportunity to be heard.

The Algorithm Behind Virality

Virality is one of the most coveted phenomena in the digital world. Whether it is a meme, a video, a news article, or a social movement, viral content spreads at an exponential rate, reaching millions of people in a short amount of time. While many believe that virality is purely a matter of luck, the truth is that social media algorithms play a crucial role in determining which content gains traction and which disappears into obscurity. Behind every viral post is a sophisticated algorithm designed to analyze engagement, user behavior, and network effects to maximize content distribution. Understanding how these algorithms work provides insight into why certain content spreads rapidly while other posts, despite high-quality production, fail to gain visibility.

Virality begins with engagement. Social media algorithms prioritize content that receives immediate interactions, such as likes, comments, shares, and watch time. The first few minutes or hours after a post is published are crucial in determining whether it will go viral. Platforms monitor how quickly users engage with the content, and if a post shows strong early performance, the algorithm pushes it to a larger audience. This initial boost creates a feedback loop: the more engagement a post receives, the more the algorithm amplifies it, exposing it to an even broader audience. This process continues as long as engagement remains high, allowing content to snowball into virality.

The type of engagement also matters. Not all interactions are weighted equally in an algorithm's ranking system. A share carries more weight than a like because it indicates that the content is compelling enough for a user to distribute it to their own network. Comments, especially long or meaningful ones, signal a deeper level of engagement, suggesting that the post has sparked a conversation. Watch time is a critical factor for video content, with algorithms favoring videos that are viewed to completion rather than those that are skipped or abandoned early. Platforms like TikTok and YouTube have mastered this ranking system, prioritizing content that keeps users engaged for longer durations.

Another key factor in virality is network dynamics. Content does not go viral in isolation; it spreads through interconnected user networks. If a post gains traction within a small but highly engaged group, it is more likely to be pushed to larger circles. Influencers, celebrities, and highly followed accounts play a crucial role in this process. When a viral trend is picked up by someone with a large following, it accelerates the spread of the content to a mainstream audience. Platforms recognize these influential accounts and often prioritize their posts, increasing their reach even further. This is why many brands and content creators aim to have their content shared by key influencers, knowing that a single repost can exponentially boost visibility.

The structure of the content itself also affects its viral potential. Certain formats and styles are more likely to be favored by algorithms. Short, attention-grabbing videos, emotionally charged headlines, and visually appealing images have a higher chance of being promoted. Algorithms are optimized to detect patterns in successful content and replicate those patterns across different users. If a specific video format is performing well, platforms may recommend similar videos to users who have engaged with that type of content before. This explains why viral trends often emerge in clusters, with multiple variations of the same theme appearing across different accounts.

Emotional appeal is another critical component of virality. Content that triggers strong emotions—whether positive or negative—tends to generate higher engagement. Posts that inspire awe, laughter, outrage, or empathy are more likely to be shared than neutral or informational content. Social media algorithms have been trained to recognize these emotional triggers, prioritizing content that elicits strong reactions. This is why sensationalized news headlines, humorous memes, and emotionally compelling stories often outperform purely informational posts. The algorithm amplifies what people react to most intensely, reinforcing emotional engagement as a key driver of virality.

Context and timing play a crucial role in determining whether content goes viral. Trends emerge based on real-world events, cultural moments, and seasonal interests. A post that aligns with a major news story, a social movement, or a trending meme has a much higher chance of spreading quickly. Social media platforms track real-time engagement patterns to identify emerging trends, adjusting their algorithms to prioritize content that aligns with what users are currently interested in. This creates a competitive environment where timing is everything. A post made too early may go unnoticed, while one made too late may be buried under newer, more relevant content. Successful content creators and marketers study algorithmic patterns to determine the optimal time to post based on peak engagement hours and trending discussions.

Algorithmic amplification can also create a snowball effect, where content gains momentum far beyond its original reach. Once a post reaches a critical mass of engagement, it is often featured in trending sections, recommended feeds, or explore pages. This further accelerates its spread, exposing it to users who may not have been part of the original audience. Platforms like Instagram and Twitter have dedicated sections for trending topics, where high-engagement posts are showcased for millions of users. This additional layer of algorithmic boosting ensures that viral content reaches a much larger audience than it would through organic sharing alone.

Despite the power of algorithms in driving virality, external factors such as media coverage and offline events can further amplify content. News outlets, blogs, and mainstream media often pick up viral social media trends, giving them an additional push beyond the platform's algorithm. This cross-platform amplification helps transform online moments into widespread cultural phenomena. Brands and marketers capitalize on these viral moments by creating reactive content, joining conversations, and leveraging the algorithm to keep their content at the forefront of trending discussions.

Virality is not always positive. Just as uplifting and entertaining content can go viral, so can misinformation, controversy, and harmful trends. The same algorithms that promote engaging content do not inherently distinguish between factual information and falsehoods. Misinformation often spreads faster than factual content because it is designed to be shocking and attention-grabbing. Social media platforms have introduced fact-checking systems and content moderation measures to combat the spread of misleading information, but the fundamental mechanics of virality remain unchanged. Content that provokes strong reactions will always have a higher chance of being amplified, whether it is accurate or not.

As algorithms continue to evolve, the science of virality will become even more refined. Platforms will likely introduce new ranking factors, integrate AI-driven personalization, and further optimize engagement prediction models. Understanding these changes is crucial for content creators, brands, and users who want to navigate the digital landscape effectively. The forces that drive virality are deeply embedded in the structure of social media, making it one of the most powerful phenomena shaping online interactions. Whether intentional or accidental, the spread of viral content is dictated by a combination of algorithmic design, human psychology, and network effects, creating an ever-changing digital ecosystem where content can rise to global visibility in a matter of hours.

Recommendation Systems: From TikTok to YouTube

Recommendation systems are the driving force behind content discovery on social media platforms, determining what users see and shaping their digital experiences. Unlike chronological feeds that display content in the order it was posted, modern platforms rely on sophisticated algorithms to personalize recommendations based on user behavior. These systems analyze vast amounts of data, tracking interactions such as watch time, likes, shares, and search history to predict what content will keep users engaged. Platforms like TikTok and YouTube have mastered recommendation algorithms, creating an environment where users can endlessly scroll through content curated specifically for them. These recommendation systems not only dictate individual content experiences but also influence cultural trends, creator success, and the spread of information on a global scale.

TikTok has emerged as one of the most effective platforms when it comes to personalized recommendations. Unlike older social media models that rely heavily on user-selected follows and subscriptions, TikTok's For You Page is almost entirely algorithm-driven. Instead of showing users content from people they actively follow, TikTok prioritizes videos that align with their engagement patterns. The algorithm begins learning about a user's preferences from the moment they open the app, analyzing how long they watch a video, whether they swipe past it quickly, and how they interact with it through likes, comments, and shares. This rapid feedback loop allows TikTok to deliver highly relevant content almost instantly, making the platform addictive and encouraging users to spend hours scrolling through endless personalized recommendations.

One of the key components of TikTok's recommendation system is its ability to detect micro-trends and push them to the forefront of user feeds. The platform monitors how small clusters of users interact with new content and determines whether it has the potential to go viral. If an emerging trend receives high engagement from an initial test group, TikTok's algorithm rapidly scales its reach, exposing it to a broader audience. This is why viral challenges, dances, and memes spread so quickly on TikTok compared to other platforms. The system does not rely on large influencers to dictate trends but instead allows content from smaller creators to gain traction based on engagement metrics alone. This democratization of virality has made TikTok an attractive platform for new creators, as anyone has the potential to reach millions of viewers regardless of follower count.

While TikTok's recommendation system is primarily designed for short-form content, YouTube has developed a more complex system to handle a vast library of long-form videos. YouTube's algorithm is centered around two main areas: suggested videos and the homepage recommendations. Suggested videos appear in the sidebar or autoplay queue, guiding users toward related content based on their watch history, engagement, and content preferences. The homepage recommendations, on the other hand, curate a personalized feed of videos before a user even searches for anything, predicting what they will find interesting based on past behavior.

Watch time is one of the most critical factors in YouTube's recommendation system. Unlike TikTok, where short engagement bursts dictate content visibility, YouTube prioritizes videos that keep users watching for extended periods. The algorithm evaluates not only how long users watch a video but also how frequently they return to similar content. If a user watches an entire 20-minute video and then clicks on another video from the same creator or topic, the system recognizes this pattern and adjusts future recommendations accordingly. This emphasis on watch time has led to the rise of longer, more in-depth content on YouTube, as creators optimize their videos to maximize retention.

User interaction also plays a significant role in shaping YouTube's recommendations. Comments, likes, and shares contribute to the algorithm's understanding of content relevance, but not all engagement is treated equally. A video with a high number of dislikes or polarizing comments can still be recommended if it maintains strong watch time metrics. Controversial content often benefits from this dynamic, as heated discussions and debates keep users engaged and lead to more recommendations. YouTube has made efforts to limit the spread of misleading or harmful content by adjusting its algorithm to downrank videos that receive widespread fact-checking or reports, but engagement remains the dominant factor in determining recommendations.

Both TikTok and YouTube use recommendation systems to create a continuous loop of content consumption, but they differ in how they introduce new content to users. TikTok excels at serendipitous discovery, exposing users to videos they might not have actively searched for but are likely to enjoy. This creates an experience where users are constantly discovering new creators, trends, and interests without needing to manually explore. YouTube, by contrast, leans heavily on a combination of user searches and past viewing history, meaning recommendations are more predictable and based on established preferences. While YouTube does push trending content and emerging creators, its recommendation system is generally more structured around existing behaviors rather than rapid exposure to new content.

The monetization models of TikTok and YouTube also influence their recommendation strategies. YouTube's revenue model is heavily dependent on ad placements within videos, which incentivizes the platform to prioritize longer content that allows for multiple ad insertions. This explains why YouTube often promotes videos with longer runtimes and high retention rates, as they generate more revenue per view. TikTok, on the other hand, relies on a mix of short ad placements, brand partnerships, and in-app purchases, allowing it to prioritize rapid content turnover without needing extended watch durations. The different monetization priorities between the two platforms shape how their algorithms recommend content and influence user engagement strategies.

One of the most significant concerns surrounding recommendation systems is their potential to create filter bubbles and echo chambers. By continuously serving users content that aligns with their existing interests and behaviors, these algorithms can reinforce biases and limit exposure to diverse viewpoints. TikTok and YouTube both face criticism for how their recommendation systems can lead users down rabbit holes of increasingly extreme or niche content. A user who watches a few conspiracy theory videos, for example, may find themselves inundated with similar recommendations, reinforcing their beliefs rather than presenting balanced perspectives. Both platforms have attempted to mitigate these effects by adjusting algorithms to promote varied content, but engagement-driven recommendations inherently favor content that aligns with user preferences rather than challenging them.

Recommendation systems are not just shaping individual content consumption but also influencing culture, politics, and entertainment. The algorithms that power TikTok and YouTube determine which voices are amplified, which trends dominate public discourse, and how people engage with information. As these platforms continue to evolve, their recommendation systems will become even more sophisticated, incorporating artificial intelligence, real-time behavioral analysis, and new engagement metrics. The ability to predict and influence user behavior at such a massive scale raises ethical questions about the power of algorithms in shaping public opinion and digital experiences. Understanding how these systems work is essential for both creators and consumers navigating the ever-changing landscape of online content.

The Psychology of Social Media Feeds

Social media feeds are designed to capture and retain user attention by delivering a continuous stream of content that feels personalized and engaging. The psychology behind how these feeds function is deeply rooted in human behavior, leveraging cognitive biases, reward systems, and emotional triggers to keep users scrolling. Every time a user interacts with their feed, whether by liking a post, watching a video, or commenting on a discussion, they reinforce patterns that algorithms use to refine their future experience. These algorithms are built to predict what will hold a user's attention for the longest period, ensuring they stay engaged with the platform. By understanding the psychological principles that shape social media feeds, it becomes clear why these platforms are so addictive and how they influence emotions, opinions, and behaviors on a subconscious level.

One of the most powerful psychological forces behind social media feeds is variable reinforcement, a concept rooted in behavioral psychology. This principle, often compared to slot machines, suggests that unpredictable rewards create the most addictive behaviors. When a user refreshes their feed, they do not know what content they will see next, whether it will be exciting, surprising, or disappointing. This unpredictability triggers the brain's reward system, releasing dopamine each time a user encounters engaging content. The more unpredictable the reward, the more the user feels compelled to keep scrolling, hoping to experience another moment of satisfaction. This cycle leads to excessive time spent on social media, as users chase the next interesting or emotionally engaging post.

Emotional engagement is another critical factor in how feeds are structured. Social media algorithms prioritize content that evokes strong emotions, whether positive or negative, because emotional content generates higher engagement rates. Posts that trigger laughter, outrage, admiration, or sadness are more likely to be liked, commented on, and shared. This emotional amplification creates a digital environment where extreme reactions become the norm, as content that elicits neutral or moderate responses is less likely to be promoted. Over time, users become accustomed to encountering emotionally charged content, which can shape their perception of reality and influence how they react to news, cultural events, and social issues.

Confirmation bias plays a significant role in how social media feeds affect user psychology. People naturally seek out information that aligns with their existing beliefs while avoiding content that challenges their perspectives. Social media algorithms reinforce this tendency by curating feeds based on past interactions, showing users content that they are most likely to engage with. If a person frequently interacts with political opinions, entertainment trends, or lifestyle choices that match their worldview, their feed will continue to prioritize similar content. This creates echo chambers where users are rarely exposed to opposing viewpoints, leading to greater ideological polarization and a reduced ability to critically evaluate different perspectives.

The fear of missing out, or FOMO, is another psychological mechanism that keeps users engaged with social media feeds. The real-time nature of these platforms means that new content is constantly appearing, and users feel the need to stay updated to avoid missing important conversations, trends, or events. Notifications, trending hashtags, and algorithmic recommendations reinforce this urgency, making users feel that if they are not actively checking their feeds, they might miss out on something valuable. This fear drives compulsive social media use, leading to behaviors such as constantly refreshing feeds, checking notifications, and engaging in discussions simply to stay relevant within their digital communities.

Social comparison is another major psychological factor that shapes how users interact with their feeds. Social media platforms create an environment where people are continuously exposed to curated versions of others' lives, often showcasing achievements, exciting experiences, and idealized self-representations. This can lead to negative self-perception as users compare their own lives to the seemingly perfect images presented online. Research has shown that prolonged exposure to highly curated social media content can contribute to feelings of inadequacy, anxiety, and depression, particularly among younger users who are more susceptible to social validation. Algorithms that prioritize visually appealing, high-engagement content further exacerbate this issue by ensuring that polished, aspirational content dominates feeds, reinforcing unrealistic social norms and expectations.

Another psychological factor influencing social media feeds is the concept of cognitive ease. People are more likely to engage with content that is easy to process and understand rather than information that requires deep thinking or effort. This is why social media favors short videos, quick headlines, and bite-sized content that can be consumed effortlessly. The preference for easily digestible content means that nuanced discussions, in-depth analysis, and complex ideas often struggle to gain visibility compared to simpler, more emotionally charged content. This phenomenon contributes to the oversimplification of news, social issues, and cultural conversations, as platforms prioritize content that maximizes engagement rather than content that promotes critical thinking.

The illusion of choice is another factor influencing how social media feeds manipulate user behavior. While users may feel like they are actively choosing what to engage with, the reality is that their options are pre-selected by algorithms that determine what content appears in their feed. The more a user interacts with a particular type of content, the more the algorithm reinforces that preference, narrowing the diversity of information they encounter. This creates a sense of personalization while simultaneously limiting exposure to new ideas, unfamiliar perspectives, and diverse content. As a result, users often mistake their algorithmically curated feeds for a broad representation of reality when, in fact, they are only seeing a filtered subset of available content.

Social validation is another psychological driver of social media engagement. Likes, comments, and shares act as social currency, providing users with immediate feedback on their thoughts, opinions, and self-expression. This feedback loop conditions users to seek approval from their digital audience, reinforcing behaviors that generate positive engagement. When a post receives high levels of interaction, it signals to the user that their content is valued, encouraging them to continue posting similar material. Conversely, when a post receives little engagement, it can lead to feelings of rejection or invisibility. The desire for social validation influences what users choose to share, how they present themselves online, and the types of interactions they prioritize within their digital communities.

The constant stream of content presented in social media feeds can also lead to information overload. With an endless supply of posts, videos, and updates, users often struggle to process and retain information effectively. The overwhelming nature of continuous scrolling can lead to cognitive fatigue, where users passively consume content without critically engaging with it. This passive consumption reduces the ability to discern credible information from misinformation, as the sheer volume of content makes it difficult to evaluate sources and context. Social media platforms capitalize on this by optimizing feeds for engagement rather than comprehension, prioritizing quick interactions over meaningful understanding.

Social media feeds are not just a reflection of user preferences; they are carefully engineered systems designed to maximize engagement by leveraging human psychology. By tapping into cognitive biases, emotional triggers, and social validation mechanisms, platforms ensure that users remain engaged for as long as possible. These algorithms shape the way people perceive the world, interact with information, and form opinions. Understanding the psychological principles that drive social media feeds provides insight into why these platforms are so compelling and why they have such a profound impact on individual behavior and societal dynamics.

Manipulating Algorithms: Bots, Clickbait, and Hacks

Social media algorithms are designed to optimize engagement by curating content that keeps users active on a platform for as long as possible. However, these algorithms are not immune to manipulation. Various actors, from individual influencers to large-scale organizations, exploit weaknesses in these systems to boost visibility, spread misinformation, and drive profits. By leveraging bots, clickbait tactics, and algorithmic hacks, these manipulators can distort online discourse, influence public opinion, and artificially amplify certain narratives. As social media platforms struggle to combat these tactics, the constant cat-and-mouse game between algorithm designers and those attempting to exploit them continues to evolve.

Bots are among the most pervasive tools used to manipulate social media algorithms. These automated accounts are programmed to behave like real users, generating engagement signals that trick platforms into believing that certain content is more popular than it actually is. Bots can be used to artificially inflate the number of likes, shares, and comments on a post, making it appear more credible and increasing the likelihood that the algorithm will promote it to a wider audience. Political groups, marketing agencies, and even governments have used bot networks to amplify messages, create artificial trends, and influence conversations by overwhelming real users with coordinated activity. By flooding comment sections with repetitive messages, bots can also create the illusion of public consensus, making certain viewpoints appear more widely accepted than they actually are.

Clickbait is another common strategy used to manipulate algorithms. Social media platforms prioritize content that receives high engagement, and nothing captures attention faster than a sensationalized headline or misleading thumbnail. Clickbait tactics rely on provoking curiosity, outrage, or excitement to encourage users to click on a post, often leading them to content that does not match their expectations. This method is frequently used by online publishers, influencers, and advertisers looking to maximize traffic and ad revenue. Clickbait works because social media algorithms often do not measure content quality, only interaction metrics. As long as users are clicking, liking, and sharing, the algorithm will continue to push clickbait content to more people, regardless of its accuracy or value.

The rise of engagement farming has further contributed to the spread of low-quality, manipulative content. Engagement farms are networks of fake accounts or real users who are paid to interact with specific posts to boost their visibility. By coordinating mass interactions, these groups can trick social media algorithms into ranking certain content higher in feeds and recommendation systems. This practice is particularly prevalent in influencer marketing, where accounts seeking rapid growth purchase likes, followers, and comments to appear more popular. While many platforms have attempted to crack down on fake engagement, engagement farming remains a widespread tactic used to game the system.

Algorithmic hacks, also known as growth hacks, involve exploiting platform mechanics to gain an unfair advantage in visibility and reach. These hacks can range from exploiting loopholes in ranking systems to using automated scripts that artificially inflate engagement. One common growth hack is the use of engagement pods, where groups of users agree to like, comment, and share each other's posts to boost their collective visibility. These pods take advantage of algorithmic preferences for high-engagement content, making it appear as though certain posts are naturally gaining traction when they are actually being artificially promoted. Another growth hack involves keyword stuffing, where content creators overload descriptions, tags, and captions with trending terms to trick the algorithm into categorizing their content as highly relevant, even when it is not.

Misinformation campaigns often leverage multiple algorithmic manipulation tactics simultaneously to spread false narratives. By using a combination of bots, clickbait headlines, and engagement farming, bad actors can rapidly amplify misleading content, ensuring that it reaches large audiences before fact-checkers can intervene. The spread of misinformation is particularly problematic during elections, global crises, and public health emergencies, where manipulated algorithms can shape public perception in ways that have real-world consequences. While social media platforms have implemented measures to combat misinformation, the sheer speed at which false content spreads often outpaces moderation efforts, allowing manipulated narratives to gain traction before they can be debunked.

Another method of algorithmic manipulation involves exploiting trending topic algorithms. Many social media platforms have dedicated sections for trending content, which are determined by algorithms that analyze real-time engagement. By coordinating activity through bots or engagement pods, manipulators can artificially push certain topics onto trending lists, increasing their visibility and credibility. Once a topic trends, it often gains additional organic traction as real users start discussing it, further reinforcing its spread. This technique has been used to promote political propaganda, brand campaigns, and even hoaxes that otherwise would not have gained widespread attention.

Social media companies have responded to these manipulation tactics by refining their algorithms and implementing stricter moderation policies. AI-driven detection systems are now used to identify bot activity, fraudulent engagement, and spam-like behavior. Platforms have also introduced measures such as downranking clickbait content, flagging misleading posts, and verifying accounts to reduce the impact of fake engagement. Despite these efforts, manipulators continuously adapt, finding new ways to exploit algorithmic weaknesses. The rapid evolution of AI and machine learning means that algorithmic manipulation will always be an ongoing challenge, requiring platforms to constantly update their detection and prevention mechanisms.

Ethical concerns surrounding algorithmic manipulation highlight the broader issue of how social media platforms prioritize engagement over content quality. Many of the tactics used to exploit algorithms stem from the way these platforms are designed to reward high interaction rates, regardless of whether the engagement is genuine or artificially generated. The emphasis on metrics such as watch time, shares, and likes creates an environment where those who understand how to game the system can achieve outsized influence, often at the expense of more authentic voices. As a result, social media feeds are frequently dominated by content optimized for manipulation rather than meaningful discourse.

The impact of algorithmic manipulation extends beyond digital spaces, influencing journalism, politics, and business. Traditional media outlets now compete with clickbait-driven digital content for attention, while political campaigns must navigate a landscape where social media manipulation can distort public debates. Brands and influencers face pressure to engage in algorithmic hacks just to remain competitive in an environment where organic reach is increasingly difficult to achieve. The ability to manipulate algorithms has become a critical skill for those looking to succeed in the digital space, raising questions about the long-term sustainability of a system that rewards strategic exploitation over genuine engagement.

The arms race between platforms and manipulators will continue as both sides develop increasingly sophisticated techniques to outmaneuver one another. Social media companies will need to balance the need for engagement-driven algorithms with safeguards against exploitation, while users must become more aware of how their interactions shape the visibility of content. Algorithmic manipulation is not just a technical issue; it is a fundamental challenge that affects how information is distributed, who gets heard, and what narratives dominate public discourse. Understanding the mechanisms behind bots, clickbait, and hacks is essential for navigating an online world where visibility is often determined not by merit, but by who knows how to game the system most effectively.

The Economics of Social Media Algorithms

Social media platforms are not just communication tools; they are multi-billion-dollar businesses driven by advertising revenue and data monetization. At the core of these business models are algorithms that determine what content users see, how long they stay engaged, and which ads they are most likely to interact with. Social media companies rely on these algorithms to maximize user retention and engagement because the longer a user stays on the platform, the more advertising opportunities can be generated. The economics of social media algorithms is deeply intertwined with user behavior, data collection, and the competition for attention in an increasingly digital economy.

The primary source of revenue for social media platforms is advertising. Companies pay to have their ads placed in users' feeds, stories, videos, and recommended content. However, not all advertising is equally effective, which is why platforms use sophisticated algorithms to target users with highly personalized ads. These algorithms analyze user data, including browsing history, likes, shares, and time spent on different types of content, to predict what kind of advertisements will generate the highest engagement. The more precisely an algorithm can match an ad to a user's interests, the higher the likelihood that the user will click on it, generating revenue for both the advertiser and the platform. This economic incentive has led social media companies to refine their algorithms continuously, ensuring that they deliver the most relevant and engaging content to keep users interacting with the platform.

Data is the most valuable asset in the social media economy. Every action a user takes—every click, comment, or pause while scrolling—is recorded and analyzed. This data allows platforms to build detailed profiles of users, which are then used to optimize both organic content recommendations and targeted advertising. The ability to predict user behavior with high accuracy makes social media platforms incredibly attractive to advertisers, who can reach specific demographics with personalized messaging. This data-driven advertising model is far more effective than traditional media advertising, where companies had to rely on broad demographic assumptions rather than precise behavioral insights. Because of this, advertisers are willing to pay premium prices for access to the highly segmented audiences that social media platforms offer.

The competition for user attention is one of the defining economic forces behind social media algorithms. Since advertising revenue is tied to engagement, platforms are designed to keep users scrolling for as long as possible. This is why algorithms prioritize content that maximizes watch time, interaction, and emotional engagement. Content that generates strong reactions—whether positive or negative—is more likely to be promoted because it keeps users engaged and encourages further interactions. The more time users spend on a platform, the more ads they see, increasing the platform's revenue. This model explains why engagement-driven algorithms often prioritize sensational, polarizing, or emotionally charged content, as these types of posts are more likely to capture attention and drive discussions.

The rise of influencer marketing has further shaped the economic landscape of social media algorithms. Brands and businesses increasingly rely on social media personalities to promote products, taking advantage of their large, engaged audiences. Influencers, in turn, must optimize their content for algorithmic visibility, ensuring that their posts receive high engagement to remain relevant in the platform's ranking system. This has led to a shift in content strategies, where influencers tailor their posts to fit algorithmic preferences, often using tactics such as engagement bait, viral trends, and emotionally compelling storytelling. The economic success of influencers depends on their ability to work within the constraints of social media algorithms, making algorithm mastery a critical skill for digital content creators.

Monetization models vary across different platforms, but they all depend on engagement as the key metric for financial success. YouTube, for example, generates revenue through ads placed within videos, rewarding creators who produce long-form content that maximizes watch time. TikTok, on the other hand, integrates advertising through sponsored content and brand partnerships, encouraging creators to participate in trends that align with advertiser interests. Instagram and Facebook monetize primarily through paid promotions and in-feed advertising, ensuring that their algorithms prioritize content that keeps users scrolling and interacting. Each platform fine-tunes its algorithm to maximize profitability, balancing user satisfaction with advertiser demands.

Subscription-based models are emerging as an alternative to traditional ad-driven revenue, but they still rely on algorithmic engagement. Platforms like Twitter (now X) and YouTube offer premium memberships that remove ads and provide exclusive content, but even these services use recommendation algorithms to keep users engaged. The logic remains the same: the more time a user spends on the platform, the more valuable they are, whether through direct payments or increased exposure to sponsored content. Even subscription platforms like Patreon and OnlyFans, which operate outside traditional social media ecosystems, rely on algorithmic discovery to help creators attract new subscribers and sustain their income.

Algorithmic ranking systems have also given rise to concerns about economic inequality in content distribution. Small businesses, independent creators, and new influencers often struggle to gain visibility in an environment where algorithms favor already-popular content. Since engagement history plays a significant role in ranking, established accounts with high engagement rates are more likely to continue receiving algorithmic promotion, while new accounts may remain invisible unless they go viral. This creates a feedback loop where those who already have large followings continue to grow, while those without an initial audience struggle to gain traction. Some platforms offer paid promotions as a way to bypass organic ranking limitations, allowing businesses and creators to pay for increased visibility. However, this further reinforces the economic divide, as those with larger budgets can secure more exposure while those with limited resources remain algorithmically disadvantaged.

The ethical implications of engagement-driven algorithms have led to increasing scrutiny from regulators and the public. Critics argue that the relentless pursuit of engagement prioritizes profit over user well-being, encouraging addictive behaviors, misinformation, and divisive content. Governments and advocacy groups have called for greater transparency in how algorithms function, pushing for regulations that require social media companies to disclose how content is ranked and monetized. Some proposals suggest limiting data collection, enforcing stricter ad-targeting policies, and holding platforms accountable for algorithmic bias. While social media companies have implemented some changes, such as giving users more control over their feed preferences, the economic incentives behind engagement-driven algorithms remain a powerful force shaping online experiences.

As social media continues to evolve, new economic models will emerge, but the fundamental relationship between algorithms and monetization will persist. The competition for attention will drive platforms to refine their recommendation systems, advertisers will seek new ways to target audiences, and content creators will continue adapting their strategies to fit algorithmic preferences. Understanding the economics behind social media algorithms provides insight into why certain types of content dominate feeds, why user data is so valuable, and why platforms are designed to maximize engagement above all else. The business of social media is built on the foundation of algorithmic optimization, ensuring that every scroll, click, and interaction serves the financial interests of the platforms that shape the digital landscape.

Advertisements, Targeting, and Data Collection

Social media platforms have become some of the most powerful advertising machines in history, revolutionizing the way businesses connect with consumers. Unlike traditional advertising models that rely on broad demographic assumptions, social media advertising is built on precision targeting, made possible by extensive data collection. Every interaction a user has on a platform is recorded, analyzed, and used to refine advertising strategies, ensuring that ads reach the people most likely to engage with them. The business model of social media is deeply intertwined with this system, as platforms generate the majority of their revenue by selling targeted advertising opportunities to companies looking to maximize their marketing impact.

At the core of social media advertising is the ability to target users based on detailed behavioral data. Platforms track an extensive range of user activities, including likes, comments, shares, watch history, search queries, and even time spent on certain types of content. This data allows advertisers to create hyper-specific audience segments, reaching people based on their interests, purchasing behavior, location, and even predicted future actions. Instead of casting a wide net, advertisers can direct their campaigns toward users who have already demonstrated an interest in similar products or services, dramatically increasing conversion rates and return on investment.

The data collection process begins the moment a user signs up for a social media account. Basic profile information, such as age, gender, location, and language preferences, is immediately stored and used to build an initial advertising profile. As users interact with content, the algorithm refines this profile, identifying patterns and predicting preferences with increasing accuracy. Over time, the system becomes highly sophisticated, categorizing users into thousands of micro-segments based on their digital behavior. These segments allow advertisers to target niche groups with extreme precision, from fitness enthusiasts who engage with weight-loss content to travelers who frequently search for vacation deals.

One of the most effective forms of targeting is retargeting, which involves showing ads to users who have previously interacted with a brand or visited a specific website. This strategy is made possible through tracking technologies such as cookies and pixel tracking, which follow users across different websites and social media platforms. If a user visits an online store but does not make a purchase, they are likely to see ads for that exact product on their social media feeds in the following days. Retargeting has been proven to significantly increase the likelihood of conversion because it keeps the product top-of-mind and encourages users to complete their transactions.

Social media platforms also enable lookalike audience targeting, a technique that allows advertisers to find new customers who share characteristics with their existing customer base. By analyzing patterns in user behavior, engagement history, and purchasing habits, the algorithm identifies potential customers who are statistically likely to be interested in a brand's offerings. This method is widely used by businesses to expand their reach without wasting resources on broad, ineffective advertising. Lookalike targeting ensures that ads are only shown to users who closely match the profile of existing customers, increasing the efficiency of marketing campaigns.

Another key aspect of social media advertising is native advertising, where promotional content is seamlessly integrated into users' feeds. Unlike traditional banner ads, which are often ignored or blocked, native ads blend in with organic content, making them feel less intrusive and more engaging. Sponsored posts on Instagram, promoted tweets on Twitter, and in-feed video ads on TikTok all use this approach to capture user attention without disrupting the browsing experience. Native advertising is particularly effective because it leverages the same engagement-driven algorithms that promote regular content, ensuring that ads reach users who are most likely to interact with them.

The massive scale of data collection and targeted advertising has raised concerns about user privacy and data security. Many users are unaware of the extent to which their personal information is being collected, stored, and monetized. While platforms claim to anonymize data before selling it to advertisers, the sheer volume of collected information makes it possible to create highly detailed profiles of individual users. Data breaches and unauthorized access to user information have further heightened concerns, leading to growing demands for stricter privacy regulations and greater transparency in how platforms handle user data.

Regulatory bodies have taken steps to address privacy concerns, introducing laws such as the General Data Protection Regulation (GDPR) in Europe and the California Consumer Privacy Act (CCPA) in the United States. These regulations require companies to disclose what data they collect, how it is used, and provide users with the option to opt out of certain types of tracking. While these measures have increased awareness about data privacy, they have not significantly disrupted the core business model of social media advertising, as most users continue to accept terms of service agreements without fully understanding their implications.

In response to privacy concerns, some platforms have introduced tools that allow users to control how their data is used for advertising. Facebook and Instagram, for example, offer settings where users can see why they are being targeted by certain ads and adjust their preferences. Google provides options to disable personalized ads, and Apple has implemented App Tracking Transparency (ATT), which requires apps to ask for user permission before tracking their activity across different platforms. Despite these efforts, the vast majority of users do not actively modify their settings, meaning that personalized advertising remains highly effective and continues to generate billions in revenue for social media companies.

The future of targeted advertising is likely to involve even more advanced artificial intelligence and machine learning models. Predictive analytics will allow advertisers to anticipate user needs before they even express them, creating hyper-personalized experiences that feel almost intuitive. Voice and facial recognition technology, combined with AI-driven behavioral analysis, may further refine ad targeting, making recommendations based on tone of voice, facial expressions, and real-time emotional states. While these advancements promise more relevant and engaging advertisements, they also raise ethical questions about the limits of surveillance and the potential for manipulation.

As social media advertising continues to evolve, the balance between effective marketing and user privacy will remain a central issue. Platforms will seek new ways to optimize ad delivery while complying with increasing regulatory scrutiny. Users will need to become more aware of how their data is collected and take proactive steps to protect their privacy if they wish to limit targeted advertising. The economics of social media are fundamentally built on data collection and precision targeting, ensuring that as long as these platforms exist, the relationship between advertisements, targeting, and user data will remain a defining force in the digital landscape.

The Role of AI in Content Moderation

Content moderation is one of the most critical and challenging tasks for social media platforms, ensuring that harmful, offensive, or illegal content does not spread unchecked. As the volume of user-generated content continues to grow at an unprecedented scale, artificial intelligence has become an essential tool in helping platforms detect and manage problematic material. AI-driven moderation systems are designed to scan billions of posts, images, videos, and comments in real-time, flagging or removing content that violates platform guidelines. While these systems have significantly improved the efficiency of content moderation, they also raise concerns about accuracy, bias, and the potential for overreach in limiting free expression.

The core function of AI in content moderation is pattern recognition. Machine learning models are trained on vast datasets of labeled content, allowing them to identify text, images, and videos that match known patterns of harmful material. These models rely on natural language processing (NLP) to analyze text-based content, determining whether a comment, caption, or post contains hate speech, threats, or misinformation. Similarly, AI-powered image and video recognition systems scan visual content for nudity, graphic violence, or copyrighted material. The more data these systems process, the more refined their detection capabilities become, enabling them to identify problematic content with increasing accuracy.

One of the most widely used applications of AI in content moderation is the detection of hate speech. Social media platforms employ machine learning algorithms to analyze text for offensive language, racial slurs, and inflammatory rhetoric. These models consider not only individual words but also the broader context of a conversation to determine whether a post should be flagged. However, hate speech detection remains a complex challenge due to the nuances of language, cultural differences, and evolving slang. AI systems can struggle to distinguish between genuine hate speech and posts that use similar language in a non-offensive context, such as satire or educational discussions. This limitation has led to cases where legitimate content is mistakenly removed while harmful content slips through undetected.

Another major role of AI in content moderation is combating misinformation and disinformation. Social media platforms use AI-driven fact-checking tools to analyze news articles, viral posts, and user-generated content for misleading or false claims. These systems compare information against verified sources, flagging content that contradicts established facts. When AI detects potential misinformation, it may reduce the visibility of the post, add a warning label, or direct users to fact-checked sources. While this approach helps limit the spread of false information, it is not foolproof. Misinformation often evolves rapidly, making it difficult for AI systems to keep up with emerging narratives. Additionally, some users distrust fact-checking initiatives, viewing them as biased or politically motivated, which complicates efforts to combat misinformation effectively.

AI also plays a crucial role in identifying and removing harmful content such as child exploitation, graphic violence, and terrorist propaganda. Platforms employ AI-powered detection systems to scan uploads in real-time, blocking or reporting material that matches known harmful content. These systems are particularly effective in recognizing explicit imagery and violent videos, as they can compare new uploads against large databases of previously identified harmful content. However, AI moderation in this area must strike a balance between rapid detection and the risk of over-censorship, as some content related to news reporting, historical documentation, or human rights activism may contain graphic elements but serve an important public interest.

Spam and automated bot activity are also major concerns that AI helps address. Machine learning models detect patterns of spam behavior, such as accounts that post repetitive messages, engage in mass-following tactics, or use suspicious engagement methods. AI-powered moderation systems can automatically block or limit the reach of these accounts, preventing them from flooding social media with low-quality or manipulative content. While this is an effective strategy for reducing spam, it has also led to false positives, where legitimate users or businesses have been mistakenly flagged as spam and had their accounts restricted.

AI moderation extends beyond detecting harmful content; it also influences algorithmic ranking decisions. Platforms use AI to downrank posts that contain borderline policy violations, ensuring that such content does not receive as much visibility. This means that even if a post is not explicitly removed, AI can limit its reach by preventing it from appearing in search results, recommendations, or trending sections. This method of content suppression, often referred to as shadowbanning, has been controversial, as users are not always aware when their content is being restricted. Critics argue that AI-driven downranking can disproportionately affect certain communities, particularly when moderation biases exist within the training data.

One of the most persistent challenges in AI content moderation is bias. Machine learning models are only as good as the data they are trained on, and if that data contains biases, the AI will reflect them. Studies have shown that AI systems may disproportionately flag content from certain demographics while allowing similar content from other groups to remain online. For example, automated moderation tools have been found to unfairly target African American Vernacular English (AAVE) as offensive while allowing similar language in other contexts. Similarly, LGBTQ+ content has been mistakenly classified as inappropriate due to outdated training data that associates discussions of sexuality with adult content. These biases can lead to uneven enforcement of moderation policies, affecting marginalized communities more than others.

AI moderation also struggles with context-dependent content, such as satire, irony, and coded language. Many online discussions use humor, sarcasm, or cultural references that AI models have difficulty interpreting. A phrase that is offensive in one context may be harmless or even empowering in another. Human moderators are often required to review AI-flagged content to determine its true intent, but the sheer volume of content means that platforms rely heavily on automated systems. This can lead to situations where content is unfairly removed while genuinely harmful material remains online due to AI limitations.

The ongoing development of AI content moderation seeks to improve accuracy, fairness, and transparency. Platforms are experimenting with hybrid models that combine AI detection with human review to minimize false positives and negatives. Some companies are investing in more diverse training datasets to reduce bias, while others are introducing appeal mechanisms that allow users to challenge automated moderation decisions. The goal is to create moderation systems that can effectively manage harmful content while preserving freedom of expression and ensuring fair enforcement of policies.

Despite its limitations, AI is an indispensable tool in content moderation, helping platforms manage the overwhelming scale of online activity. As technology advances, AI-driven moderation systems will continue to evolve, incorporating more sophisticated natural language understanding, real-time contextual analysis, and adaptive learning models. The challenge will be ensuring that these systems are transparent, accountable, and capable of distinguishing between harmful content and legitimate expression. Social media platforms will need to refine their approaches to moderation, balancing the need for AI automation with the importance of human judgment in cases where context and nuance are essential.

The Battle Between Organic Reach and Paid Promotions

Social media has evolved from a space of personal connections and community engagement into a highly competitive digital marketplace where visibility is increasingly dictated by financial investment. At the heart of this transformation lies the ongoing struggle between organic reach and paid promotions. Organic reach refers to the ability of content to gain visibility and engagement naturally, without the aid of paid advertising. Paid promotions, on the other hand, involve businesses and individuals spending money to boost their content and reach a wider audience. As platforms continue to prioritize revenue generation, organic reach has declined, forcing brands, influencers, and content creators to adapt to an ecosystem where paid promotions are often necessary for visibility.

In the early days of social media, organic reach was the primary way content spread. Users saw posts from friends, family, and followed pages in chronological order, ensuring that content reached its intended audience without interference from algorithms. Businesses and creators could build communities and engage directly with followers without needing to invest in advertising. However, as social media platforms grew in popularity, the volume of content became overwhelming. To manage this influx, platforms introduced algorithms designed to curate feeds based on engagement metrics, relevance, and user behavior. While these changes improved the user experience by filtering out low-quality content, they also made it harder for organic content to reach large audiences.

The decline of organic reach became particularly evident on platforms like Facebook, where algorithm updates significantly reduced the visibility of posts from business pages and publishers. Studies showed that organic reach for brand pages dropped to single-digit percentages, meaning that even highly engaged audiences saw only a fraction of the content from the pages they followed. Instagram and Twitter followed similar patterns, adjusting their ranking systems to prioritize content that generated the highest engagement. While these changes encouraged meaningful interactions, they also created an environment where content creators had to work harder than ever to maintain visibility.

As organic reach declined, paid promotions became the primary method for brands and businesses to ensure their content was seen. Social media platforms introduced a variety of paid advertising options, including sponsored posts, boosted content, and targeted ad campaigns. These paid promotions allowed users to reach specific demographics, ensuring that their content appeared in the feeds of potential customers or followers. Unlike organic reach, which relied on unpredictable algorithmic factors, paid promotions provided a guaranteed level of visibility in exchange for financial investment. This shift fundamentally changed the dynamics of content distribution, making social media an increasingly pay-to-play environment.

The rise of paid promotions has led to an imbalance in content visibility, where those with larger advertising budgets have a distinct advantage over smaller creators and businesses. Large corporations can allocate significant resources to paid campaigns, ensuring that their content appears prominently in users' feeds. Independent creators, small businesses, and startups, on the other hand, often struggle to compete in an environment where organic reach is limited, and paid advertising is costly. This disparity has led to concerns that social media platforms are favoring commercial interests over authentic content, prioritizing revenue generation at the expense of organic community engagement.

Despite the challenges, organic reach is not entirely obsolete. Certain types of content still have the potential to go viral or gain traction without paid promotion. Platforms like TikTok have maintained an algorithmic structure that allows smaller creators to gain visibility based on engagement rather than follower count or ad spend. The For You Page on TikTok prioritizes content that resonates with users, giving new creators the opportunity to reach massive audiences without the need for paid advertising. YouTube also offers a level of organic discoverability through its recommendation algorithm, rewarding videos with high watch time and audience retention. While organic reach is not as powerful as it once was, strategic content creation and engagement tactics can still help creators achieve visibility without relying solely on paid promotions.

One of the key strategies for maximizing organic reach is understanding and adapting to algorithmic preferences. Platforms prioritize content that encourages interactions, meaning that posts with high engagement—likes, comments, shares, and watch time—are more likely to be pushed to wider audiences. Content creators and brands often use engagement-driven tactics, such as asking questions, using trending hashtags, and participating in viral challenges, to increase their chances of appearing in users' feeds. Consistency in posting, high-quality visuals, and storytelling elements also contribute to better organic performance. However, even with these strategies, organic reach remains inconsistent and difficult to predict, making paid promotions an attractive option for those seeking reliable visibility.

Paid promotions offer several advantages that organic reach cannot guarantee. Businesses and content creators can use precise targeting options to reach specific audiences based on demographics, interests, and online behavior. This level of customization ensures that ads are shown to users who are most likely to engage with the content, increasing the chances of conversion or follower growth. Retargeting campaigns allow advertisers to re-engage users who have previously interacted with their content, reinforcing brand awareness and driving repeat engagement. The ability to track performance metrics in real-time also makes paid promotions a valuable tool for optimizing marketing strategies and maximizing return on investment.

The growing reliance on paid promotions has led to a shift in the way brands and influencers approach content creation. Instead of focusing solely on organic engagement, many creators now incorporate paid strategies into their overall marketing plans. Influencers often collaborate with brands through sponsored content, integrating advertisements into their posts in a way that feels authentic to their audience. Brands use a combination of organic content and paid promotions to build credibility while ensuring that their most important messages reach a wide audience. This hybrid approach allows businesses and creators to balance the unpredictability of organic reach with the reliability of paid visibility.

As social media platforms continue to refine their algorithms and advertising models, the relationship between organic reach and paid promotions will continue to evolve. While organic reach remains valuable for community building and audience engagement, paid promotions have become an essential tool for those looking to expand their visibility in a crowded digital landscape. The challenge for content creators and businesses is finding the right balance between the two, leveraging organic strategies to foster authentic connections while using paid promotions strategically to ensure consistent reach. Understanding the dynamics of this battle is crucial for anyone looking to succeed in the modern social media ecosystem, where visibility is no longer guaranteed but must be actively earned.

The Influence of Influencers: How Algorithms Favor Certain Users

Social media influencers have become some of the most powerful figures in digital culture, shaping consumer behavior, political discourse, and entertainment trends. While platforms promote the idea that anyone can achieve success through organic growth and audience engagement, the reality is that algorithms play a significant role in determining which influencers gain visibility and which struggle to be seen. The mechanisms that drive social media ranking systems are designed to prioritize content that maximizes engagement and retention, often creating an ecosystem where certain users receive outsized influence while others are left competing for algorithmic attention. Understanding how algorithms favor specific users provides insight into the power dynamics of the influencer economy and the barriers to success for new creators trying to break through.

The first way algorithms favor certain influencers is by reinforcing engagement loops. Once an account gains traction and starts receiving high engagement, platforms are more likely to promote its content to a wider audience. This creates a cycle where successful influencers continue growing exponentially, while newer or smaller creators struggle to reach visibility. Since social media platforms prioritize content that keeps users engaged for long periods, they tend to favor accounts that have already demonstrated their ability to retain audience attention. The result is a system where established influencers maintain dominance, while new creators must find ways to hack the algorithm or rely on external promotion to gain recognition.

Engagement metrics are one of the primary drivers of algorithmic favoritism. Influencers who consistently receive high levels of likes, shares, comments, and watch time are more likely to have their content pushed to the top of feeds and recommendation systems. This means that influencers who already have a loyal audience benefit from the algorithm's natural tendency to prioritize engaging content. Additionally, platforms reward content that sparks conversations, whether through controversial takes, relatable experiences, or viral challenges. The influencers who understand how to craft content that generates discussion have a much higher chance of being favored by ranking algorithms, further increasing their visibility.

Watch time has become an increasingly important factor in algorithmic favoritism, especially on video-based platforms like YouTube and TikTok. Influencers who create content that keeps users watching for extended periods are more likely to have their videos recommended. This has led to the rise of certain video formats, such as reaction videos, long-form discussions, and serialized storytelling, as creators optimize their content for maximum retention. The algorithmic emphasis on watch time means that influencers who already have an engaged audience are at an advantage because their followers are more likely to watch their content in full, signaling to the algorithm that their videos should be promoted further.

Brand partnerships and monetization opportunities also contribute to algorithmic favoritism. Social media platforms are businesses, and they benefit from influencers who attract advertising revenue. Influencers who collaborate with brands, participate in sponsored campaigns, or generate high ad revenue for the platform are often favored in content ranking systems. Platforms want to keep advertisers happy, which means prioritizing creators who have a strong track record of monetizable engagement. This creates an uneven playing field where influencers with established brand deals are more likely to receive algorithmic boosts, while smaller creators struggle to reach a level where monetization becomes viable.

The relationship between influencers and platform-specific initiatives further reinforces algorithmic favoritism. Platforms frequently promote certain types of content based on their strategic goals, and influencers who align with these priorities benefit from increased exposure. For example, when Instagram launched Reels to compete with TikTok, it heavily promoted influencers who adopted the format early, rewarding them with algorithmic visibility. Similarly, YouTube has prioritized YouTube Shorts, boosting creators who focus on short-form video content. Influencers who recognize these shifts and quickly adapt to platform priorities often receive an algorithmic advantage, allowing them to grow faster than those who stick to older content formats.

Algorithmic favoritism is also influenced by social validation. When an influencer reaches a certain level of popularity, their content is perceived as more authoritative, entertaining, or valuable simply because of their existing follower count. This creates a bandwagon effect, where users are more likely to engage with content from influencers they recognize or trust. Algorithms take these engagement signals as proof that the content is high-quality, reinforcing the cycle of visibility for already successful influencers. This phenomenon makes it difficult for new creators to break into the influencer economy, as users are naturally drawn to established personalities while algorithms reinforce their dominance.

Influencer networks and collaborations further strengthen algorithmic favoritism. Large influencers often collaborate with one another, sharing audiences and cross-promoting content. This collaboration strategy benefits both parties, as each influencer gains exposure to the other's followers. Since engagement is the primary driver of algorithmic ranking, these shared audiences contribute to higher levels of interaction, signaling to the platform that the influencers involved should be prioritized in recommendations. Smaller creators who lack access to these networks often struggle to gain visibility, as they do not have the same collaborative advantages that more established influencers enjoy.

Certain demographics and content styles also receive algorithmic favoritism, either intentionally or unintentionally. Platforms have been criticized for disproportionately promoting influencers who fit specific aesthetic standards, such as conventionally attractive individuals or creators who appeal to mainstream cultural preferences. Studies have shown that beauty filters, professional editing, and high-production content often receive more algorithmic promotion than raw or unpolished content. This has led to concerns about inclusivity, as creators from underrepresented backgrounds often find it harder to gain algorithmic traction. While platforms claim to prioritize diverse voices, the reality is that algorithmic biases often mirror societal biases, making it harder for certain groups to achieve visibility.

Despite the barriers, some influencers manage to break through without algorithmic favoritism by leveraging external factors such as viral trends, community-driven engagement, or strategic content marketing. Niche creators who focus on highly specific topics or unique content styles can sometimes bypass traditional algorithmic limitations by cultivating dedicated audiences that actively promote their work. Platforms like TikTok have made it easier for new creators to gain visibility through a recommendation system that occasionally pushes unknown accounts into the For You Page, but even on these platforms, long-term success often requires adapting to algorithmic preferences.

The way algorithms favor certain influencers shapes the broader digital landscape, determining which voices dominate online conversations and which struggle to be heard. While platforms claim to offer equal opportunities for growth, the reality is that algorithmic structures inherently benefit those who already have a strong engagement base, monetization opportunities, and strategic alignment with platform priorities. Understanding how these systems work is crucial for anyone looking to navigate the world of social media influence, as success is not just about creating great content but also about mastering the algorithmic forces that dictate visibility and reach.

Algorithmic Censorship: Who Decides What You See?

Social media platforms have become the primary spaces for public discourse, but the content that appears in a user's feed is far from neutral. Every post, video, and comment is subject to algorithmic filtering, determining what is promoted, suppressed, or removed altogether. This invisible process is known as algorithmic censorship, where machine learning models decide what content is visible and what disappears from public view. Unlike traditional censorship, which is typically carried out by governments or media regulators, algorithmic censorship operates through complex automated systems designed by private corporations. These algorithms determine the flow of information on a massive scale, shaping political discussions, cultural trends, and personal beliefs without users fully understanding the extent of their influence.

At the core of algorithmic censorship is the concept of content moderation. Social media platforms enforce community guidelines to prevent the spread of harmful material such as hate speech, misinformation, and violent content. AI-powered moderation systems scan billions of posts daily, flagging content that violates these guidelines. While the goal of these systems is to create safer online environments, the process is not always transparent. Users often find their posts removed, accounts restricted, or content shadowbanned without clear explanations. The lack of visibility into how these decisions are made raises concerns about fairness, accountability, and potential bias in the enforcement of moderation policies.

One of the primary ways algorithmic censorship occurs is through automated content removal. AI models trained on large datasets detect and delete posts that match predefined criteria for harmful or inappropriate content. Platforms rely on these systems to handle the sheer volume of posts uploaded every second, as human moderators alone cannot keep up. However, these automated systems are far from perfect. They often struggle to interpret context, leading to false positives where harmless content is incorrectly flagged while genuinely harmful content remains undetected. Satire, political speech, and discussions of sensitive topics frequently fall victim to these errors, raising questions about the effectiveness and fairness of AI-driven moderation.

Another form of algorithmic censorship is downranking, where platforms do not remove content outright but instead limit its visibility. This can happen when a post is flagged for containing controversial, misleading, or borderline policy-violating material. Instead of appearing prominently in user feeds or search results, the content is pushed lower in rankings, reducing engagement and limiting its reach. Users are often unaware that their content has been deprioritized, as there is rarely an explicit notification. This silent suppression technique is controversial because it allows platforms to control narratives without direct censorship, influencing which ideas gain traction and which fade into obscurity.

Shadowbanning is another method of algorithmic censorship that frustrates users and creators alike. When a user is shadowbanned, their content is still technically available but is not actively promoted by the algorithm. This means fewer people see their posts, engagement drops dramatically, and their ability to grow an audience is hindered. Platforms rarely acknowledge when shadowbanning occurs, leaving users to speculate about why their content is receiving less visibility. Activists, independent journalists, and marginalized communities have frequently reported experiencing shadowbanning, raising concerns that algorithmic censorship disproportionately affects certain voices while allowing more mainstream or commercially favorable content to flourish.

Political content is especially vulnerable to algorithmic censorship. During elections, protests, or major global events, platforms often adjust their moderation policies to combat misinformation, extremism, or foreign interference. While these efforts are intended to protect democratic processes, they sometimes result in legitimate political speech being restricted. Social media companies have been accused of bias, either suppressing conservative viewpoints or limiting progressive activism, depending on the platform and the region. The opacity of these moderation decisions fuels distrust, with users questioning whether platforms are acting impartially or exerting influence over political discourse.

Censorship of news and media outlets also occurs through algorithmic decisions. News organizations rely on social media for traffic and audience engagement, but changes in ranking systems can drastically impact their visibility. Platforms frequently update their algorithms to prioritize content from specific sources while downranking others, influencing which news stories gain prominence. Independent journalists and smaller news organizations often struggle to compete with major outlets that have stronger relationships with tech companies. Algorithmic censorship in the news industry raises ethical concerns about who controls information flow and whether social media companies should have the power to determine which news stories receive attention.

Bias in algorithmic censorship is another critical issue. AI moderation systems are trained on datasets that may reflect cultural biases, leading to uneven enforcement of content policies. Research has shown that certain dialects, languages, and cultural expressions are more likely to be flagged as inappropriate, while similar content from other groups goes unnoticed. For example, African American Vernacular English (AAVE) has been disproportionately targeted by automated moderation systems, and LGBTQ+ content has been mistakenly labeled as adult or sensitive material. These biases reinforce existing inequalities, limiting visibility for certain communities while favoring others.

The economic incentives behind algorithmic censorship further complicate the issue. Social media platforms generate revenue through advertising, and brands do not want their ads appearing next to controversial or divisive content. To maintain advertiser relationships, platforms use aggressive content moderation strategies to ensure that brand-safe content is prioritized. This means that posts discussing controversial but important topics, such as climate change, human rights, or systemic injustice, may receive less algorithmic promotion because they carry a higher risk of advertiser discomfort. The financial motivations behind censorship raise questions about whether platforms are truly moderating content for the benefit of users or simply protecting their business interests.

The lack of transparency in algorithmic censorship fuels frustration and conspiracy theories among users. Without clear explanations for why content is removed, downranked, or shadowbanned, people speculate about hidden agendas and political bias. Some users believe that platforms are actively silencing dissenting opinions, while others argue that social media companies are too lax in moderating harmful content. The truth is often somewhere in between, as platforms struggle to balance free expression with content moderation while managing commercial pressures.

Efforts to address algorithmic censorship have been met with mixed results. Some platforms have introduced content appeals processes, allowing users to challenge moderation decisions, but these systems are often slow and inconsistent. Others have implemented transparency reports detailing content removals and enforcement actions, but these reports rarely provide the full picture of how algorithms influence visibility. Governments and regulatory bodies have begun investigating social media censorship practices, but there is no global consensus on how to balance content moderation with the right to free speech.

Algorithmic censorship shapes the digital landscape, determining what information is accessible and which voices are amplified or silenced. While content moderation is necessary to maintain safe online spaces, the opacity and biases of these systems raise concerns about fairness, representation, and the centralization of power in the hands of tech companies. As social media continues to evolve, the debate over who decides what users see will remain one of the most pressing challenges in the digital age.

How Social Media Affects Mental Health

Social media has transformed the way people connect, communicate, and consume information, but its impact on mental health is a topic of increasing concern. While platforms offer opportunities for self-expression, support networks, and entertainment, they also introduce psychological stressors that can contribute to anxiety, depression, and other mental health challenges. The constant exposure to curated lifestyles, the pressure to gain validation through likes and comments, and the addictive nature of algorithm-driven engagement have all played a role in shaping mental well-being in the digital age. Understanding how social media affects mental health requires examining its influence on self-esteem, social comparison, addiction, sleep patterns, and overall emotional well-being.

One of the most significant ways social media affects mental health is through social comparison. Users are constantly exposed to highlight reels of others' lives, filled with carefully curated images, achievements, and moments of happiness. This creates a distorted reality where individuals compare their everyday experiences to an unrealistic standard of success and perfection. The pressure to present an idealized version of oneself can lead to feelings of inadequacy, self-doubt, and low self-esteem. People who frequently compare themselves to others on social media are more likely to experience dissatisfaction with their own lives, even if the content they are consuming does not reflect reality.

The validation-seeking nature of social media further intensifies these feelings. Likes, comments, and shares serve as digital markers of approval, reinforcing the idea that social value is tied to online engagement. Many users experience anxiety when their posts do not receive the expected level of attention, leading to self-doubt and a fear of rejection. The anticipation of receiving likes can trigger dopamine releases in the brain, similar to the effects of gambling or other addictive behaviors. This creates a cycle where users continuously post content in pursuit of validation, becoming increasingly dependent on social media for self-worth. The unpredictability of engagement makes the experience even more addictive, as users are drawn to checking their accounts repeatedly for updates on their online performance.

The addictive nature of social media is another factor that negatively impacts mental health. Platforms are designed to maximize user engagement, using endless scrolling, autoplay features, and algorithmic recommendations to keep people online for as long as possible. These design elements exploit the brain's reward system, making it difficult for users to disengage. Excessive social media use has been linked to increased stress, decreased productivity, and difficulty focusing on real-world tasks. Many individuals struggle with compulsive checking behaviors, feeling the need to constantly refresh their feeds even when they are not actively engaged in meaningful interactions. Over time, this leads to reduced attention spans, decreased motivation, and a sense of digital fatigue.

Sleep disturbances are another significant consequence of excessive social media use. Many people use social media late at night, exposing themselves to blue light emitted by screens, which disrupts melatonin production and interferes with sleep cycles. The habit of checking social media before bed can lead to insomnia, restless sleep, and decreased overall sleep quality. Additionally, emotionally charged content—whether it be distressing news, online arguments, or personal insecurities—can heighten anxiety levels, making it difficult to relax before sleep. Poor sleep has a direct impact on mental health, contributing to increased stress, irritability, and reduced cognitive function.

Cyberbullying and online harassment have also become major mental health concerns associated with social media use. Unlike traditional bullying, which is confined to physical spaces, online harassment can be relentless, following victims across multiple platforms and invading their personal spaces. Negative comments, threats, and public shaming can lead to severe emotional distress, social withdrawal, and, in extreme cases, suicidal ideation. Young people are particularly vulnerable to cyberbullying, as their developing sense of self is more easily influenced by negative online interactions. The anonymity of the internet often emboldens users to engage in harmful behavior without facing real-world consequences, exacerbating the problem.

Misinformation and sensationalized content contribute to increased stress and anxiety levels among social media users. Constant exposure to negative news, conspiracy theories, and fear-based narratives can create a sense of helplessness and paranoia. The phenomenon of doomscrolling, where users compulsively consume distressing news for prolonged periods, has been linked to heightened anxiety and depression. Social media algorithms often prioritize emotionally charged content, leading to an information environment that feels overwhelmingly negative. This constant exposure to fear-inducing material can alter a person's perception of reality, making the world seem more dangerous or unstable than it actually is.

Despite these negative effects, social media can also provide positive mental health benefits when used mindfully. Online communities offer support networks for individuals struggling with mental health issues, allowing them to connect with others who share similar experiences. Many people find solace in digital spaces where they can openly discuss their struggles without fear of judgment. Mental health professionals, advocacy groups, and wellness influencers use social media to spread awareness, provide resources, and encourage conversations about mental well-being. The accessibility of these resources has helped many individuals find coping strategies, support groups, and even professional help that they might not have sought out otherwise.

The impact of social media on mental health varies depending on how it is used. While excessive engagement, social comparison, and online toxicity can lead to negative outcomes, intentional and mindful usage can create opportunities for connection, self-expression, and personal growth. Recognizing the signs of unhealthy social media habits—such as compulsive checking, emotional distress tied to online interactions, or disruptions in daily life—can help individuals take steps to regain control over their digital experiences. Setting boundaries, limiting screen time, curating a positive feed, and engaging in offline activities are some ways to mitigate the negative effects of social media on mental health.

As social media platforms continue to evolve, addressing their impact on mental health will remain a crucial challenge. Companies are beginning to implement features such as time management tools, content warnings, and algorithmic adjustments to promote healthier digital habits. However, the responsibility also falls on users to be mindful of their online behavior and recognize when their social media use is negatively affecting their well-being. By understanding the psychological mechanisms at play, individuals can make more informed choices about how they engage with social media, ensuring that their digital experiences contribute to, rather than detract from, their mental health.

The Ethics of Social Media Algorithms

Social media algorithms are among the most influential technological forces shaping human behavior, determining what content people see, what ideas gain traction, and how online interactions unfold. While these algorithms are designed to optimize engagement, retain users, and drive advertising revenue, they also raise significant ethical concerns. The way they influence public discourse, manipulate emotions, and prioritize profit over well-being has sparked debates about corporate responsibility, data privacy, and the unintended consequences of algorithmic decision-making. Understanding the ethical implications of social media algorithms is crucial as platforms continue to evolve and integrate artificial intelligence into everyday digital interactions.

One of the primary ethical concerns surrounding social media algorithms is their role in amplifying misinformation. Engagement-driven ranking systems prioritize content that generates strong reactions, whether positive or negative. This has led to the widespread dissemination of false or misleading information, as sensationalized content is more likely to capture user attention. Studies have shown that misinformation often spreads faster than factual reporting because it is designed to provoke strong emotional responses. The ethical dilemma arises from the fact that social media companies profit from engagement, even when the content being promoted contributes to confusion, public distrust, or real-world harm. While platforms have introduced fact-checking measures and content moderation policies, these efforts often lag behind the rapid spread of viral misinformation, leaving ethical questions about the responsibility of tech companies in shaping public knowledge.

Another major ethical issue is the creation of filter bubbles and echo chambers. Social media algorithms are designed to show users content that aligns with their interests and past behaviors. While this personalization enhances user experience, it also reinforces ideological divisions by exposing individuals primarily to content that confirms their existing beliefs. This contributes to political and social polarization, as users are less likely to encounter diverse perspectives or engage in critical thinking. The ethical concern lies in the fact that algorithms shape reality for each individual in a way that may limit exposure to balanced viewpoints, reinforcing biases and deepening societal divisions. Many argue that social media companies have an obligation to design algorithms that promote informational diversity rather than reinforcing homogenous thought bubbles.

The exploitation of human psychology for engagement maximization presents another ethical dilemma. Social media platforms are designed to be addictive, using techniques such as infinite scrolling, autoplay, and notification systems to keep users engaged for as long as possible. These features are rooted in behavioral psychology, leveraging dopamine-driven reward mechanisms to create compulsive usage patterns. The ethical question is whether it is justifiable for companies to design platforms that encourage excessive screen time, particularly among younger users who are more susceptible to digital addiction. Critics argue that tech companies have a responsibility to prioritize user well-being over profit-driven engagement metrics, implementing features that promote healthy digital habits rather than exploiting psychological vulnerabilities.

Privacy and data ethics are also central concerns in the discussion of social media algorithms. Platforms collect vast amounts of personal data to refine their recommendation systems and improve ad targeting. This data includes browsing history, location tracking, purchase behavior, and even inferred personality traits. While companies argue that data collection enhances user experience by making content more relevant, it also raises ethical questions about consent, transparency, and the potential for abuse. Many users are unaware of the extent to which their data is being used to shape their online experiences, and there is often little transparency about how algorithms make decisions based on this data. The potential for data misuse, including the unauthorized sale of user information and the risk of surveillance, further complicates the ethical landscape of social media algorithms.

Algorithmic bias is another ethical challenge that has significant societal implications. AI-driven content moderation, ranking, and recommendation systems are only as fair as the data they are trained on. If training datasets contain biases—whether racial, gender-based, or political—these biases become embedded in the algorithm itself. This has led to instances where certain communities or viewpoints are disproportionately suppressed, while others receive algorithmic preference. For example, studies have shown that automated moderation systems may unfairly flag content from marginalized groups, while allowing similar content from other demographics to go unmoderated. The ethical responsibility of social media companies is to ensure that their algorithms do not reinforce existing inequalities, but achieving unbiased AI remains a complex and ongoing challenge.

The monetization of social media engagement further complicates ethical considerations. Platforms rely on targeted advertising as their primary source of revenue, which means that their algorithms are optimized not just for user engagement, but also for advertiser interests. This raises questions about whether social media companies prioritize corporate profit over the well-being of their users. Advertisers benefit from algorithms that track user behavior with extreme precision, allowing for hyper-personalized marketing that can be both persuasive and manipulative. Ethical concerns arise when these targeting mechanisms are used for predatory practices, such as exploiting vulnerable users, spreading political propaganda, or promoting unhealthy behaviors. The line between ethical advertising and digital manipulation is increasingly blurred, leading to calls for greater regulation of algorithmic ad targeting.

The issue of content censorship and free speech is another ethical debate surrounding social media algorithms. Automated moderation systems determine which posts are removed, downranked, or shadowbanned, shaping the boundaries of acceptable discourse online. While platforms have a responsibility to combat hate speech, harassment, and misinformation, the opaque nature of algorithmic enforcement often leads to concerns about fairness and bias. Some users feel that social media companies have too much power in deciding what speech is acceptable, while others argue that platforms are not doing enough to prevent harmful content. The ethical challenge is finding a balance between maintaining free expression and ensuring that online spaces remain safe and non-toxic.

The responsibility of social media companies in mitigating the negative effects of their algorithms is a topic of ongoing debate. Some platforms have introduced measures to promote digital well-being, such as time management tools, content warnings, and options to see more diverse perspectives. However, many of these changes are reactive rather than proactive, implemented only after public pressure or regulatory scrutiny. The ethical question remains: should social media companies take a more active role in ensuring that their algorithms promote positive societal outcomes, even if it means sacrificing some level of engagement and profitability?

Government regulations and policy interventions are increasingly being considered as solutions to the ethical dilemmas posed by social media algorithms. Some countries have introduced data protection laws, algorithmic transparency requirements, and restrictions on targeted advertising to address concerns about privacy, bias, and misinformation. However, regulatory efforts face significant challenges, including resistance from tech companies, jurisdictional complexities, and concerns about government overreach. The ethical responsibility of social media companies, governments, and users themselves continues to be a point of contention as societies grapple with the long-term impact of algorithmic decision-making.

The ethics of social media algorithms touch on some of the most fundamental questions about technology, society, and human behavior. As these systems become more sophisticated and integrated into everyday life, their impact will only continue to grow. The challenge is ensuring that the immense power of algorithmic decision-making is wielded responsibly, balancing innovation and engagement with fairness, transparency, and the well-being of users. The future of social media will depend on whether platforms prioritize ethical considerations alongside their pursuit of growth, shaping a digital landscape that serves the interests of individuals and society as a whole.

The Role of Big Tech in Shaping Society

Big Tech companies have transformed nearly every aspect of modern life, influencing how people communicate, consume information, conduct business, and interact with the world around them. The rise of technology giants such as Google, Facebook (now Meta), Amazon, Apple, and Microsoft has created a digital ecosystem where a handful of corporations control vast amounts of data, economic power, and societal influence. Social media platforms, search engines, and e-commerce sites shape human behavior in ways that extend beyond simple convenience, impacting democracy, privacy, culture, and even individual psychology. As these companies continue to expand their reach, questions arise about their responsibilities, the power they wield, and the ethical considerations of their growing influence on society.

One of the most significant ways Big Tech shapes society is through its control over information flow. Search engines like Google determine what information people access by ranking search results based on complex algorithms. Social media platforms filter content through personalized feeds, deciding what news stories, opinions, and advertisements users see. These systems are not neutral; they are driven by engagement metrics, advertising revenue, and artificial intelligence models that prioritize certain types of content over others. The ability to influence what information spreads, which narratives gain traction, and how people perceive the world gives Big Tech unprecedented power over public discourse.

The political influence of Big Tech has become increasingly evident, as social media platforms play a central role in elections, activism, and political movements. The way algorithms amplify certain messages while suppressing others can shape public opinion and voter behavior. Political campaigns rely on targeted digital advertising to reach specific demographics, using data analytics to tailor messages based on individual preferences. At the same time, misinformation and political manipulation have flourished on social media, with foreign and domestic actors exploiting algorithmic weaknesses to spread propaganda, discredit opponents, and polarize societies. Tech companies have responded by implementing content moderation policies, fact-checking initiatives, and algorithmic adjustments, but these measures have sparked debates about free speech, censorship, and corporate bias in shaping political narratives.

The economic dominance of Big Tech has redefined industries, creating monopolistic environments where smaller businesses struggle to compete. E-commerce platforms like Amazon have revolutionized retail, but they have also forced small businesses to either adapt to their ecosystem or risk being overshadowed. App stores controlled by Apple and Google dictate which digital products reach consumers, charging fees and enforcing policies that give them leverage over developers. Social media platforms have become essential marketing tools for businesses, but changes in algorithmic visibility often force companies to pay for exposure rather than relying on organic reach. The concentration of economic power in the hands of a few tech giants raises concerns about market competition, innovation, and the ability of smaller players to thrive in a digital economy controlled by a few corporations.

The relationship between Big Tech and personal privacy has been a growing concern as digital platforms collect vast amounts of user data. Every click, search, purchase, and interaction is tracked, analyzed, and stored, creating detailed behavioral profiles that fuel targeted advertising. While companies argue that data collection enhances user experience by personalizing content and recommendations, it also raises questions about consent, surveillance, and data security. High-profile data breaches, whistleblower revelations, and scandals such as the Facebook-Cambridge Analytica case have exposed the risks associated with unchecked data collection. Governments have responded with regulations such as the General Data Protection Regulation (GDPR) in Europe and the California Consumer Privacy Act (CCPA), but enforcement remains a challenge as Big Tech continues to evolve its data strategies.

The cultural impact of Big Tech extends beyond economics and politics, influencing social norms, entertainment, and human behavior. Streaming services like YouTube, Netflix, and Spotify use recommendation algorithms to shape media consumption, determining which movies, music, and shows gain popularity.

Influencers and digital personalities have replaced traditional celebrities, building audiences on platforms like Instagram, TikTok, and Twitch. The way people form relationships, express themselves, and engage in cultural trends is increasingly mediated by technology companies that set the rules of engagement. This shift has led to both positive and negative consequences, enabling new forms of creativity and global connectivity while also fostering issues like digital addiction, online harassment, and the erosion of privacy.

Artificial intelligence and automation, driven by Big Tech innovation, are reshaping the workforce and the future of employment. AI-powered systems now handle tasks that were once performed by humans, from customer service chatbots to automated journalism and machine learning-driven hiring processes. While automation increases efficiency and reduces costs, it also raises concerns about job displacement, economic inequality, and the ethical implications of AI decision-making. Big Tech companies play a central role in the development and deployment of AI technologies, influencing everything from healthcare diagnostics to facial recognition surveillance. The potential for AI to both empower and exploit society depends on how these technologies are designed, regulated, and integrated into everyday life.

The role of Big Tech in education has also expanded, particularly with the rise of online learning platforms, digital textbooks, and AI-driven tutoring systems. Tech companies have partnered with schools and universities to provide educational tools, but this has also sparked concerns about data privacy and the commercialization of education. The increasing reliance on digital learning raises questions about accessibility, as students from lower-income backgrounds may not have the same access to technology as their wealthier counterparts. The intersection of technology and education highlights both the opportunities and inequalities created by the growing influence of Big Tech in shaping the future of learning.

As Big Tech continues to push the boundaries of innovation, ethical considerations become more urgent. The balance between technological advancement and societal well-being is a delicate one, requiring accountability, regulation, and corporate responsibility. Governments, advocacy groups, and the public are demanding greater transparency from tech companies, calling for clearer policies on data usage, algorithmic decision-making, and the mitigation of harmful content. At the same time, tech companies argue that innovation should not be stifled by excessive regulation, as technological progress has the potential to solve global challenges in healthcare, climate change, and connectivity.

The debate over Big Tech's role in society is far from settled. As these companies continue to expand their influence, the decisions they make—whether in shaping online speech, controlling access to information, or redefining economic structures—will have long-term consequences for individuals and institutions alike. The challenge lies in ensuring that technological progress benefits society as a whole, rather than concentrating power in the hands of a few corporations. The future of digital governance, ethical technology development, and corporate accountability will determine whether Big Tech remains a force for innovation or a growing source of societal concerns.

Algorithms and Free Speech: A Delicate Balance

The rise of social media has redefined the concept of free speech, shifting the landscape of public discourse from traditional institutions to algorithmically driven platforms. Unlike newspapers, television, or radio, which rely on human editors and regulatory oversight, social media platforms use artificial intelligence to determine what content is promoted, what is suppressed, and what is removed entirely. This shift has raised profound questions about the balance between freedom of expression and the need to moderate harmful content. As algorithms take on the role of digital gatekeepers, concerns about censorship, bias, misinformation, and the influence of corporate interests have become central to discussions on the future of online speech.

Social media companies often portray themselves as neutral platforms, emphasizing that they provide a space for users to express their ideas freely. However, the reality is that algorithms shape online conversations in ways that are far from neutral. These systems are designed to prioritize engagement, ensuring that users remain on the platform for as long as possible. In doing so, they tend to amplify emotionally charged content, controversial opinions, and highly engaging posts—regardless of their accuracy or ethical implications. While this dynamic has allowed for greater public participation in discussions that were once controlled by mainstream media, it has also led to the rapid spread of misinformation, extremist content, and digital harassment.

The role of algorithms in determining visibility has sparked debates about censorship and viewpoint suppression. When social media platforms remove or downrank content, users often accuse them of bias, arguing that their voices are being unfairly silenced. Political groups, activists, and independent journalists have reported cases where their content has been shadowbanned, demonetized, or restricted due to algorithmic decisions. While platforms insist that their moderation policies are applied evenly, critics argue that these measures disproportionately affect certain ideologies or marginalized groups. The challenge lies in distinguishing between legitimate content moderation—such as removing hate speech or harmful misinformation—and unjustified censorship that limits the free exchange of ideas.

Hate speech and extremist content pose a significant challenge in maintaining a balance between free speech and platform moderation. Social media companies have a responsibility to prevent the spread of harmful content, including hate speech, terrorism-related material, and targeted harassment. However, the line between harmful rhetoric and controversial opinions is often blurred, making it difficult to enforce policies consistently. Automated moderation systems frequently misinterpret context, flagging satire, political dissent, or discussions about social issues as violations of community guidelines. As a result, some users feel that their speech is being restricted by AI systems that lack the ability to understand nuance.

Misinformation is another key issue in the debate over algorithms and free speech. While free expression is a fundamental right, the unchecked spread of false information can have serious consequences, especially in areas such as public health, elections, and global crises.

Social media platforms have introduced fact-checking initiatives and downranking strategies to limit the reach of misleading content, but these measures have been met with resistance. Some users perceive fact-checking efforts as biased or politically motivated, leading to accusations that tech companies are acting as arbiters of truth. The question of who gets to decide what is considered misinformation remains contentious, especially when scientific understanding evolves or when political perspectives influence interpretations of facts.

Government intervention in online speech adds another layer of complexity to the debate. Some countries have pushed for regulations that require platforms to remove harmful content more aggressively, while others have accused social media companies of stifling dissent and suppressing political opposition. In some cases, authoritarian regimes have pressured platforms to take down content critical of the government, raising ethical concerns about the role of private corporations in enforcing state-imposed restrictions on speech. At the same time, democratic governments struggle with finding the right balance between regulating harmful content and upholding the principles of free expression. Laws designed to combat hate speech or misinformation often have unintended consequences, leading to the suppression of legitimate discourse.

The economic incentives behind algorithmic moderation further complicate the issue. Social media platforms generate revenue through advertising, and advertisers are unlikely to want their content placed next to controversial or divisive material. As a result, platforms have an economic motivation to limit content that could jeopardize ad revenue, leading to potential conflicts of interest in content moderation decisions. While companies claim to prioritize user safety and community standards, the reality is that their financial interests often influence how aggressively they moderate certain topics. This dynamic raises concerns about whether content suppression is driven by ethical considerations or corporate profit motives.

Transparency in algorithmic decision-making is a growing demand among free speech advocates and digital rights organizations. Many argue that platforms should provide greater insight into how content moderation decisions are made, offering clearer explanations for why certain posts are removed or downranked. The lack of visibility into these processes has fueled distrust, leading some users to believe that moderation is applied inconsistently or that algorithms are secretly suppressing certain viewpoints. Open-source moderation policies, independent audits, and appeals processes could help address these concerns, ensuring that content moderation decisions are made fairly and transparently.

Technological solutions to balance free speech and content moderation are still evolving. Some platforms are experimenting with decentralized moderation models, where users have greater control over what content they see and how it is filtered. Others are exploring AI-driven context analysis tools that can better distinguish between harmful speech and legitimate discourse. The development of more sophisticated natural language processing models could improve the accuracy of automated moderation, reducing the likelihood of false positives and ensuring that controversial but lawful speech is not unfairly restricted.

User responsibility also plays a role in maintaining a balanced online environment. While social media platforms have a duty to enforce their policies fairly, users must also be mindful of the content they engage with and share. Digital literacy initiatives, critical thinking education, and awareness campaigns about misinformation could help create a more informed online community. Encouraging users to engage in constructive discussions rather than fueling outrage-driven engagement could shift the nature of social media interactions toward more meaningful conversations.

The debate over algorithms and free speech is far from settled, and as technology continues to evolve, so will the challenges associated with digital expression. Striking the right balance between allowing open discourse and preventing harm is a complex task that requires cooperation between tech companies, policymakers, and the public. The future of online speech will depend on how well societies navigate this delicate balance, ensuring that freedom of expression remains protected while addressing the ethical and societal risks associated with algorithmic content moderation.

How Platforms Handle Hate Speech and Harassment

Social media platforms have become central to modern communication, enabling people to connect, share ideas, and participate in global conversations. However, the same digital spaces that foster discussion and community building are also breeding grounds for hate speech and harassment. Online abuse, ranging from targeted harassment campaigns to discriminatory rhetoric, has become a significant issue, prompting platforms to develop moderation systems designed to detect, prevent, and remove harmful content. While these efforts aim to create safer environments for users, they also raise concerns about censorship, bias, and the effectiveness of automated enforcement.

Platforms define hate speech as content that attacks, threatens, or dehumanizes individuals or groups based on characteristics such as race, ethnicity, religion, gender identity, sexual orientation, disability, or nationality. Harassment, on the other hand, includes persistent abusive behavior, threats, doxxing, and coordinated attacks meant to intimidate or silence individuals. To combat these issues, social media companies employ a combination of artificial intelligence, user reporting systems, and human moderation teams to identify and address violations of their community guidelines. However, these measures are far from perfect, leading to ongoing debates about their efficiency and fairness.

Artificial intelligence plays a key role in detecting and removing hate speech and harassment. Platforms use machine learning algorithms trained on vast datasets of previously flagged content to identify harmful language patterns. These systems scan text, images, and videos in real time, looking for words, phrases, or visual elements associated with hate speech. While AI moderation has significantly increased the speed at which platforms can respond to violations, it is not always accurate. Context is often lost in automated analysis, resulting in false positives, where harmless content is mistakenly removed, and false negatives, where harmful content remains undetected. Sarcasm, coded language, and evolving slang make it difficult for AI systems to interpret intent correctly, allowing some users to bypass detection while others face unfair restrictions.

Human moderation teams are used to review flagged content and make final decisions in cases where AI detection is inconclusive. These teams consist of employees or outsourced contractors who assess reported content against platform guidelines. While human moderators provide a layer of judgment that AI lacks, they are often overwhelmed by the sheer volume of content that requires review. Many moderators work under stressful conditions, exposed to disturbing material daily, which has led to concerns about their mental health and well-being. The reliance on human moderation also introduces the risk of inconsistencies in enforcement, as different teams may interpret policies differently depending on cultural, linguistic, or regional variations.

User reporting systems are another mechanism platforms use to address hate speech and harassment. Social media companies encourage users to flag content that violates guidelines, allowing for community-driven moderation. When a post or account is reported, it is typically reviewed by AI systems first, with human moderators stepping in if necessary. While user reporting can be effective in highlighting harmful content that AI may have missed, it is also vulnerable to misuse. Some users exploit the system to mass-report accounts they disagree with, leading to wrongful suspensions or content removals. This tactic, often referred to as brigading, has been used to silence activists, journalists, and marginalized communities whose content may be controversial but does not necessarily violate platform policies.

Platforms also implement warning labels, restrictions, and temporary suspensions as part of their enforcement measures. Instead of immediately banning accounts for hate speech or harassment, some companies use gradual penalties, such as limiting the visibility of posts, disabling certain features, or requiring users to delete offending content before regaining access to their accounts. This approach is intended to educate users on community guidelines while discouraging repeat violations. However, critics argue that these measures are often inconsistently applied, with high-profile users or influencers receiving lenient treatment compared to everyday users.

Permanent bans and account removals are the strictest actions platforms take against those who repeatedly engage in hate speech and harassment. High-profile cases, such as the banning of extremist figures or public figures who incite violence, have sparked intense debates about the role of social media in regulating speech. Some argue that deplatforming is necessary to prevent the spread of harmful ideologies, while others view it as an overreach that stifles free expression. The inconsistency in enforcement, where some users face immediate bans while others remain active despite repeated violations, fuels distrust in moderation policies and accusations of political or ideological bias.

The challenge of handling hate speech and harassment is further complicated by differing legal and cultural standards across countries. What constitutes hate speech in one region may be considered acceptable discourse in another. Some countries have strict laws against online hate speech, requiring platforms to remove content within specific timeframes or face penalties. Others take a more lenient approach, emphasizing free speech protections over content moderation. Social media companies must navigate these varying legal frameworks while maintaining global policies, often leading to conflicts between national regulations and platform guidelines. In some cases, governments pressure platforms to remove content critical of political leaders or policies, raising concerns about the use of hate speech policies as tools for censorship.

Many platforms have attempted to introduce proactive measures to prevent hate speech and harassment before it spreads. Some use content moderation tools that warn users when they are about to post something that may violate guidelines, encouraging them to reconsider their language. Others employ AI-driven interventions that reduce the visibility of harmful content before it gains traction. While these approaches aim to promote healthier online interactions, they are not foolproof, and determined bad actors continue to find ways to circumvent moderation efforts.

The role of influencers, celebrities, and public figures in shaping online discourse further complicates content moderation. High-profile individuals with large followings have the power to amplify harmful rhetoric, leading to coordinated harassment campaigns or real-world consequences. Some platforms have been criticized for failing to take action against influential users who violate policies, fearing backlash or loss of engagement. The reluctance to enforce rules equally across all users undermines trust in moderation systems, reinforcing perceptions that social media companies prioritize profit over user safety.

The debate over the effectiveness of current moderation efforts continues as social media platforms struggle to find the right balance between free speech and protecting users from harm. While AI and human moderators have improved the detection and removal of hate speech and harassment, no system is perfect, and enforcement remains inconsistent. Transparency in moderation decisions, better support for moderators, and clearer communication with users about policy enforcement are crucial steps toward addressing these challenges. As online spaces continue to evolve, platforms must continually refine their approaches to ensure that social media remains a space for meaningful engagement rather than a breeding ground for hostility and abuse.

The Impact of Algorithm Changes on Businesses

Social media algorithms are the invisible forces that determine what content appears in users' feeds, how often it is shown, and how widely it spreads. While these algorithms are primarily designed to enhance user experience and engagement, they also have profound consequences for businesses that rely on social media for marketing, sales, and brand visibility. When platforms like Facebook, Instagram, TikTok, and YouTube update their algorithms, the ripple effects can be massive, altering the way businesses reach their audiences and forcing them to adapt to new digital landscapes. Algorithm changes can lead to either growth or decline for businesses, depending on how well they adjust their strategies to align with the new ranking and recommendation systems.

For businesses that depend on organic reach, algorithm updates can be particularly disruptive. Organic reach refers to the ability to reach audiences without paid promotions, relying instead on content quality and user engagement. In the early days of social media, businesses could post updates and expect them to appear in the feeds of their followers. However, as platforms grew and the volume of content increased, social media companies introduced algorithmic ranking systems that prioritize content based on relevance, engagement, and platform-specific goals. These changes often lead to a decline in organic reach, forcing businesses to either pay for visibility through ads or rethink their content strategies to regain traction.

One of the most significant examples of algorithmic disruption occurred when Facebook changed its News Feed algorithm to prioritize content from friends and family over business pages and publishers. This shift drastically reduced the organic reach of brand pages, making it harder for businesses to engage with their audiences without paying for ads. Small businesses that relied on Facebook for customer interaction and brand awareness suddenly found themselves struggling to maintain visibility. Many had to invest heavily in paid promotions or explore alternative marketing channels to compensate for the decline in free exposure.

Instagram, which operates under Meta's ecosystem, has undergone similar changes, favoring video content over static images. The rise of Instagram Reels was fueled by algorithm updates that prioritized short-form video content to compete with TikTok. Businesses that traditionally relied on photo posts had to quickly adapt to video marketing, reformatting their strategies to include engaging, fast-paced visual content that aligned with the platform's shifting priorities. Those that failed to adjust saw reduced engagement, while those that embraced video saw increased reach and audience growth.

TikTok, with its unique For You Page algorithm, has created a new paradigm for businesses trying to reach consumers. Unlike other platforms, TikTok does not rely heavily on follower count to determine visibility. Instead, it prioritizes content based on watch time, engagement, and user behavior. This means that businesses, even small ones with no prior audience, can achieve viral success if they create content that resonates with the algorithm's preferences.

However, TikTok's frequent updates to its recommendation system mean that what works one month may not work the next, requiring businesses to continuously monitor trends and adjust their content strategies accordingly.

YouTube has also made algorithmic shifts that have impacted businesses, particularly those in content marketing and e-commerce. The platform prioritizes watch time, click-through rate, and session duration, favoring long-form content that keeps users engaged. Businesses that previously focused on short promotional videos had to adapt by creating educational, entertaining, or narrative-driven content to align with YouTube's preferences. The introduction of YouTube Shorts further changed the landscape, pushing businesses to adopt short-form video strategies alongside their traditional long-form content. Algorithm updates that affect search rankings and suggested videos can drastically alter a business's ability to attract views and subscribers, making YouTube's algorithm a critical factor in digital marketing success.

The unpredictability of algorithm changes poses a challenge for businesses that rely on social media as a primary marketing channel. A strategy that works well one year can become ineffective the next due to shifting platform priorities. Businesses must stay informed about algorithm updates, test new content formats, and be willing to pivot their strategies to remain competitive. Many have invested in social media analytics tools to track performance metrics, helping them understand how algorithmic changes affect their engagement and reach. Others have diversified their marketing efforts, using multiple platforms to reduce dependence on any single algorithm.

Paid advertising has become an essential tool for businesses seeking stability in an unpredictable social media environment. Since organic reach is often affected by algorithm updates, many businesses allocate budgets for sponsored posts, targeted ads, and influencer collaborations to ensure consistent visibility. Social media platforms offer advanced ad targeting options, allowing businesses to reach specific demographics, interests, and behaviors. While paid promotions provide a way to bypass algorithmic restrictions, they also require financial investment, which can be a challenge for small businesses with limited budgets. The shift toward pay-to-play models has made digital marketing more competitive, benefiting larger companies that can afford higher ad spending while making it harder for smaller businesses to gain traction organically.

Influencer marketing has also been impacted by algorithm shifts. As platforms prioritize engagement metrics, brands have increasingly partnered with influencers whose content performs well under current algorithmic trends. Influencers with high engagement rates are more likely to have their content recommended, making them valuable partners for businesses looking to reach targeted audiences. However, changes in ranking algorithms can affect influencer visibility, leading brands to frequently reassess their influencer partnerships based on shifting platform priorities.

Algorithm changes also affect customer service and direct communication between businesses and consumers. Many businesses use social media for customer inquiries, complaints, and support, but algorithmic changes can influence how visible these interactions are. For example, updates that prioritize private messages over public comments may shift how businesses handle customer interactions. Some platforms have also introduced AI-driven chatbots and automated responses, altering how businesses manage customer relationships in a digital-first landscape.

The long-term impact of algorithm changes on businesses is an ongoing challenge, requiring continuous adaptation and innovation. Companies that succeed in this environment are those that remain agile, experiment with new content formats, and leverage data-driven insights to optimize their strategies. The ability to predict trends, test different approaches, and adjust to evolving algorithms is now a fundamental skill in digital marketing.

Social media platforms will continue to evolve, introducing new ranking factors, content priorities, and engagement metrics. Businesses that rely on these platforms must remain proactive, staying ahead of changes and finding ways to align their strategies with emerging algorithmic trends. While algorithm updates can disrupt existing marketing efforts, they also create opportunities for businesses that are quick to adapt and leverage new platform features to their advantage. The ability to navigate these changes effectively will determine which businesses thrive in the ever-changing digital landscape.

Understanding Algorithm Updates and Why They Happen

Social media platforms and search engines are constantly evolving, driven by algorithm updates that reshape how content is ranked, distributed, and discovered. These updates impact everything from the visibility of posts and videos to the effectiveness of digital marketing strategies. Users, businesses, and content creators often experience sudden changes in engagement and reach, leading to frustration and speculation about why certain content gains or loses visibility overnight. Algorithm updates are not random; they are deliberate changes made to improve user experience, refine content recommendations, and address challenges such as misinformation, spam, and changing user behavior. Understanding why these updates happen and how they influence content distribution is essential for anyone who relies on digital platforms for engagement, business growth, or information dissemination.

Algorithm updates are driven by the need to enhance user experience. Social media platforms and search engines operate on a fundamental goal: keeping users engaged for as long as possible. This means delivering content that is relevant, valuable, and entertaining while filtering out content that is misleading, low-quality, or disruptive. Platforms analyze vast amounts of user data to determine which types of content generate the most positive interactions and which cause frustration or disengagement. If users consistently ignore certain types of posts, click away from videos too quickly, or report misleading information, platforms adjust their algorithms to prioritize better content. By continuously refining their ranking systems, platforms ensure that users receive a more personalized and satisfying experience, increasing retention and overall engagement.

Another major reason for algorithm updates is the battle against spam and low-quality content. Over time, digital platforms become targets for manipulation by individuals and businesses trying to game the system for profit. Tactics such as keyword stuffing, engagement farming, bot-driven likes and comments, and clickbait headlines have been used to artificially inflate content visibility. To maintain credibility and prevent their platforms from being overrun with low-quality material, companies update their algorithms to identify and penalize these manipulative tactics. This often leads to sudden drops in visibility for accounts that previously relied on exploitative methods, forcing content creators to adopt more authentic and high-quality strategies.

The rise of misinformation and harmful content has also played a significant role in algorithm changes. Platforms like Facebook, Twitter, and YouTube have faced criticism for enabling the rapid spread of false information, conspiracy theories, and extremist content. In response, they have developed algorithmic solutions that downrank misleading posts, flag content for fact-checking, and limit the reach of accounts that repeatedly share false information. These updates aim to create a more responsible digital environment while balancing the need for free expression. However, the implementation of these measures has sparked controversy, with some users arguing that algorithmic changes disproportionately suppress certain viewpoints or limit discussions on sensitive topics.

Algorithm updates are also influenced by changing content consumption habits. As user behavior evolves, platforms must adapt to remain relevant and competitive. The shift from text-based content to visual storytelling, the rise of short-form video, and the growing preference for interactive and immersive experiences have all driven changes in how content is ranked and recommended. Platforms like Instagram and Facebook have increasingly prioritized video content over static images, while YouTube has incorporated short-form videos alongside traditional long-form content. TikTok's success in creating an engaging, AI-driven discovery system has led other platforms to adjust their algorithms to compete in the fast-moving world of short-form entertainment. Each algorithm update reflects an attempt to align content distribution with what users are actively engaging with at any given moment.

Monetization and advertising strategies also play a role in algorithm changes. Social media platforms generate revenue through advertising, and their algorithms are designed to optimize ad placement in a way that benefits both users and advertisers. If users become overwhelmed with irrelevant or intrusive ads, they may disengage from the platform. Algorithm updates help refine ad targeting, ensuring that promoted content is more relevant and less disruptive to the user experience. Additionally, organic reach for business accounts is often reduced over time to encourage brands to invest in paid promotions. While these updates are framed as improvements to user experience, they also reflect a shift toward revenue-driven models that prioritize ad spending over unpaid content distribution.

The competitive landscape of social media and search engines is another factor that drives algorithm updates. Platforms must continuously innovate to stay ahead of competitors and maintain user engagement. When a new trend emerges, platforms quickly adjust their ranking systems to incorporate it. The introduction of TikTok's For You Page algorithm revolutionized content discovery, prompting platforms like Instagram and YouTube to prioritize similar recommendation models. The rise of AI-powered search tools has influenced how Google ranks search results, favoring conversational and intent-based queries over simple keyword matching. Algorithm updates are part of an ongoing effort to stay relevant in an industry where user preferences and technological advancements change rapidly.

Transparency surrounding algorithm updates is a frequent source of frustration for users and businesses. Platforms rarely disclose the full details of how their ranking systems operate, leading to speculation and uncertainty about what factors influence content visibility. Many companies provide general guidelines on best practices, such as prioritizing high-quality content, engaging with audiences, and avoiding manipulative tactics. However, because algorithms are constantly evolving, strategies that work today may become obsolete after the next update. This lack of transparency has led to an industry of digital marketers, SEO specialists, and social media consultants who analyze engagement patterns to decipher the latest algorithmic trends.

Despite the challenges posed by algorithm updates, they also create opportunities for those who understand how to adapt. Content creators and businesses that prioritize authenticity, audience engagement, and evolving content strategies are more likely to benefit from algorithmic changes. Staying informed about platform updates, experimenting with new formats, and focusing on long-term content value rather than short-term tricks can help navigate the shifting digital landscape. While algorithm updates can be disruptive, they are ultimately designed to refine the user experience, maintain content quality, and ensure the continued relevance of digital platforms in an ever-changing online world.

Shadow Profiles and Data Tracking

Social media platforms and tech companies have built their business models around data collection, using advanced tracking systems to monitor user behavior, preferences, and online activities. While most users understand that their interactions on platforms like Facebook, Instagram, Google, and TikTok are tracked, few realize that these companies also collect data on individuals who have never signed up for their services. This practice, known as shadow profiling, involves the creation of hidden profiles based on data collected from various sources, allowing platforms to track people who may have no direct interaction with their services. Combined with extensive data tracking mechanisms, shadow profiles raise concerns about privacy, consent, and the growing power of tech companies in the digital age.

Shadow profiles are created when platforms gather information about non-users from different sources, such as contacts uploaded by existing users, browsing activity across websites with embedded tracking tools, and third-party data brokers. For example, when a user grants an app access to their phone's contact list, that data is uploaded to the platform's servers, storing information about people who may have never signed up for an account. This means that even if someone has never used a social media platform, the company may still have data on them, including their name, phone number, email address, and potential social connections. These profiles remain hidden from public view but are used to improve ad targeting, refine recommendation algorithms, and expand the reach of data-driven marketing.

Data tracking goes far beyond the boundaries of social media apps. Many websites integrate tracking pixels, cookies, and fingerprinting techniques that allow tech companies to monitor user behavior even outside their platforms. Facebook's Pixel, Google's analytics tools, and other third-party trackers collect data on browsing history, purchase behavior, search queries, and even location patterns. This information is then used to build detailed profiles that categorize individuals based on their interests, habits, and likelihood of engaging with certain types of content or advertisements. Even if a person is not logged into a social media account, these trackers can still associate their activity with an existing shadow profile, further refining the platform's understanding of their behavior.

The sheer scale of data tracking allows companies to predict user preferences with incredible accuracy. By analyzing patterns in search history, purchase behavior, and social interactions, platforms can anticipate what content, products, or services a user is likely to engage with before they even express interest. This predictive capability is what powers hyper-personalized advertising, where ads seem almost eerily relevant to a user's recent thoughts or conversations. While some consumers appreciate the convenience of personalized recommendations, others view it as an invasion of privacy, raising ethical concerns about the extent to which companies should be allowed to track and profile individuals without their explicit consent.

One of the most controversial aspects of shadow profiles and data tracking is the lack of transparency. Users are often unaware that their data is being collected, let alone how it is being used. Privacy policies, while technically available, are often buried in lengthy legal documents filled with complex language that makes it difficult for the average person to understand what they are agreeing to. Even when platforms provide opt-out options for certain types of tracking, the process is often convoluted, requiring users to navigate multiple settings across different devices and services. This lack of clarity has led to increasing scrutiny from privacy advocates and regulators, pushing for greater transparency and user control over personal data.

Data breaches and leaks have further exposed the risks associated with shadow profiling. When tech companies experience security breaches, the information they have collected—including hidden data on non-users—can be exposed to hackers and malicious actors. These leaks reveal the extent of data tracking and raise concerns about how much personal information is stored without individuals' knowledge. The Facebook-Cambridge Analytica scandal, in which millions of user profiles were harvested without consent for political targeting, highlighted the dangers of unchecked data collection. Such incidents have fueled demands for stronger data protection laws and stricter oversight of how companies handle user information.

Governments and regulatory bodies have begun implementing measures to address the issues surrounding shadow profiles and data tracking. The European Union's General Data Protection Regulation (GDPR) requires companies to disclose the data they collect on users and non-users, allowing individuals to request deletion of their information. Similarly, the California Consumer Privacy Act (CCPA) grants consumers the right to know what data is being collected about them and to opt out of certain types of tracking. While these regulations have increased awareness and accountability, enforcement remains a challenge, as tech companies continue to find new ways to gather data while staying within the boundaries of legal compliance.

Despite regulatory efforts, the business model of most social media platforms remains fundamentally tied to data collection. Advertising revenue depends on the ability to deliver highly targeted ads, and the more data a company has, the more valuable its ad services become. This creates an inherent conflict between privacy and profit, where platforms have little incentive to limit data tracking unless compelled by external pressure. Even as companies introduce privacy-focused features, such as Apple's App Tracking Transparency (ATT), which requires apps to ask for user permission before tracking, many platforms seek alternative ways to gather behavioral insights, such as server-side tracking and AI-driven inference models.

For users who wish to protect their privacy, avoiding data tracking entirely is nearly impossible. However, there are steps individuals can take to minimize exposure, such as using privacy-focused browsers, disabling third-party cookies, installing ad blockers, and being selective about the permissions granted to apps. Virtual private networks (VPNs) can help obscure online activity, and encrypted messaging services provide alternatives to data-hungry communication platforms. While these measures offer some degree of protection, the reality is that most people are deeply embedded in the digital ecosystem, making complete anonymity difficult to achieve.

The debate over shadow profiles and data tracking is part of a broader conversation about the future of digital privacy. As artificial intelligence, biometric tracking, and machine learning algorithms continue to evolve, the ability of tech companies to collect and analyze personal data will only become more sophisticated. Whether through regulatory intervention, corporate responsibility, or increased user awareness, the challenge of balancing data-driven innovation with privacy rights will shape the next phase of the digital age. Users, businesses, and policymakers alike must grapple with the implications of an internet where every click, conversation, and interaction contributes to an ever-expanding digital footprint.

The Future of Social Media Algorithms

Social media algorithms have already transformed the way people consume content, interact with others, and receive information. However, as technology continues to advance, these algorithms are poised to evolve in ways that will further reshape digital experiences. The future of social media algorithms will be driven by artificial intelligence, machine learning, personalization, ethical considerations, and regulatory pressures. Platforms will continue refining their algorithms to improve user engagement, content discovery, and advertising effectiveness while addressing growing concerns over misinformation, bias, privacy, and mental health. The changes that lie ahead will redefine how people interact with digital spaces, influencing everything from entertainment and commerce to politics and social movements.

One of the most significant advancements in social media algorithms will be the increasing use of artificial intelligence. AI-driven recommendation systems are already capable of predicting user preferences with remarkable accuracy, but future iterations will become even more sophisticated. Deep learning models will enhance the ability of platforms to understand user behavior, detecting subtle patterns in interactions, emotions, and interests. Instead of simply recommending content based on past engagement, future algorithms will anticipate user needs before they are even expressed. AI-powered predictive analytics will allow platforms to deliver hyper-personalized content, creating experiences that feel seamless and intuitive. This level of personalization will make social media more engaging but also raises concerns about digital addiction and the reinforcement of filter bubbles.

Real-time content adaptation will be another key feature of future social media algorithms. Platforms will analyze user engagement in real-time, adjusting content recommendations dynamically based on immediate reactions. If a user spends more time watching a particular type of video, the algorithm will instantly adjust their feed to prioritize similar content. This shift will create an even more immersive digital experience, where algorithms continuously refine what is displayed based on moment-to-moment behaviors. While this could enhance user satisfaction, it also risks making platforms more manipulative, guiding user attention in ways that maximize time spent on the app rather than serving content that is necessarily meaningful or informative.

The role of ethical AI in social media algorithms will become increasingly important as concerns over bias, misinformation, and online harm continue to grow. Current algorithms have been criticized for amplifying divisive content, spreading false information, and reinforcing stereotypes. Future advancements will likely include more robust content verification systems, ensuring that misinformation is flagged before it can go viral. Platforms may implement AI-powered context analysis to determine whether a piece of content is misleading or lacks credible sources. These improvements will be crucial in addressing the growing demand for more responsible content moderation while preserving free expression. However, achieving this balance will remain one of the greatest challenges for social media companies, as any form of algorithmic intervention risks accusations of censorship or bias.

Another significant trend in the future of social media algorithms will be the integration of multimodal AI systems. These systems will not only analyze text-based interactions but also incorporate speech recognition, facial expression analysis, and biometric tracking. This means that platforms will be able to assess a user's mood and emotional state in real-time, adjusting content recommendations accordingly. If a user appears frustrated or disengaged, the algorithm might shift to suggesting uplifting content or entertainment. While this could enhance user experience, it also introduces profound ethical concerns about privacy and consent. The ability of social media platforms to interpret emotions and adjust content accordingly could lead to new forms of digital manipulation, influencing user moods and behaviors in ways that are not entirely transparent.

Regulation and policy changes will play a crucial role in shaping the future of social media algorithms. Governments and regulatory bodies are already exploring legislation to ensure greater transparency in algorithmic decision-making, requiring platforms to disclose how their ranking systems work and allowing users more control over their feeds. Some proposals include the right for users to opt out of algorithmic recommendations altogether, giving them the choice to view content in chronological order rather than based on AI-driven curation. Stricter data privacy laws may also limit how much personal information platforms can use to refine their algorithms, forcing companies to develop new methods for delivering relevant content without invasive data collection. These regulatory changes could redefine the relationship between users and social media, shifting power away from opaque algorithmic systems and toward greater user autonomy.

Decentralized social media models are another emerging development that could impact the future of algorithms. Instead of relying on centralized platforms controlled by a few major corporations, decentralized networks powered by blockchain technology could allow users to have more control over their data, content distribution, and algorithmic preferences. These platforms would enable individuals to choose how their feeds are curated, whether by selecting from different algorithmic models or using open-source AI systems. This approach could reduce concerns over bias and manipulation, as users would have the ability to customize their online experiences rather than being subject to a single platform's ranking system. However, decentralized platforms also present challenges in terms of moderation and security, as the lack of centralized control could make it more difficult to prevent the spread of harmful content.

The future of social media algorithms will also be shaped by the growing emphasis on mental health and digital well-being. Current recommendation systems are designed to maximize engagement, but future iterations may prioritize healthier interactions. Platforms could introduce AI-driven tools that encourage users to take breaks, reduce exposure to harmful content, and promote positive social connections. Some companies are already experimenting with features that limit doomscrolling, reduce exposure to toxic comment sections, or provide users with more control over the types of content they see. The challenge will be balancing user engagement with ethical responsibility, as platforms must find ways to sustain their business models while reducing the negative psychological impact of excessive social media use.

The integration of augmented reality and virtual reality into social media will further transform algorithmic interactions. As platforms like Meta push for the development of the metaverse, algorithms will need to adapt to 3D environments, personalized digital spaces, and interactive virtual communities. Future recommendation systems will not only suggest text and video content but also immersive experiences, guiding users toward virtual events, AI-generated environments, and social interactions within digital worlds. The shift from 2D social media feeds to fully immersive experiences will redefine how algorithms function, introducing new complexities in personalization, engagement tracking, and content moderation.

Social media algorithms will continue to evolve in ways that enhance personalization, improve content moderation, and integrate emerging technologies. However, the ethical challenges surrounding bias, privacy, and manipulation will remain central to discussions about the future of digital platforms. As AI becomes more advanced and social media experiences become increasingly immersive, the balance between user engagement and responsible algorithmic design will shape the next generation of online interactions. The decisions made by tech companies, policymakers, and users themselves will determine whether the evolution of algorithms leads to more meaningful digital experiences or further deepens the challenges associated with algorithmic control over information, behavior, and society at large.

The Rise of Decentralized Social Media Platforms

Traditional social media platforms are dominated by a few powerful corporations that control data, content distribution, and user interactions. Platforms like Facebook, Twitter, Instagram, and TikTok operate under centralized models, where all user-generated content is stored and managed by the company's servers. This centralized control has led to concerns over privacy, censorship, algorithmic bias, and data monetization. In response, a growing movement toward decentralized social media platforms has emerged, offering an alternative that prioritizes user autonomy, transparency, and data ownership. These decentralized platforms aim to disrupt the status quo by removing corporate control and placing power back in the hands of users and communities.

Decentralized social media platforms operate on blockchain technology or peer-to-peer networks, eliminating the need for a central authority to manage content and user data. Instead of relying on a single company to host and regulate discussions, these platforms distribute control among users, allowing them to interact freely without interference from corporate algorithms or moderation policies. This structure creates a more open and democratic digital environment, where users have greater control over their online presence, content visibility, and data privacy. By eliminating a central governing body, decentralized platforms seek to provide an alternative to traditional social media models that rely on advertising-driven engagement and algorithmic content curation.

One of the primary motivations behind the rise of decentralized social media is the growing concern over data privacy. Traditional platforms collect vast amounts of personal information, including browsing history, location data, interactions, and preferences. This data is then used to build detailed user profiles that fuel targeted advertising and engagement optimization. Many users feel uncomfortable with the extent of this surveillance and the lack of transparency regarding how their information is stored, shared, and monetized. Decentralized social media platforms offer a solution by giving users full control over their data, often using blockchain encryption to ensure that personal information remains private and secure. Users can choose what data to share, who has access to it, and whether they want to monetize their own content rather than allowing corporations to profit from their online activities.

Censorship and content moderation have also driven interest in decentralized social media. Centralized platforms enforce strict policies regarding what can and cannot be posted, often removing content that violates their guidelines or downranking posts that do not align with their engagement priorities. While content moderation is necessary to prevent harmful material from spreading, many users believe that current systems are inconsistent, biased, or influenced by corporate or political interests. Decentralized platforms offer an alternative by allowing communities to establish their own moderation rules rather than adhering to a single company's policies. Some decentralized networks implement decentralized autonomous organizations (DAOs), where users vote on content guidelines and enforcement measures, ensuring that moderation decisions reflect the collective interests of the community rather than the priorities of a corporation.

Monetization is another area where decentralized platforms provide a different approach. Traditional social media companies generate revenue through advertising, which means that their algorithms prioritize content that maximizes user engagement and ad impressions. This business model often leads to clickbait, sensationalism, and an emphasis on divisive or emotionally charged content. Decentralized platforms introduce new monetization models that allow users to earn directly from their content without relying on ads. Blockchain-based platforms enable creators to receive cryptocurrency payments, microtransactions, or token-based rewards for their contributions. This decentralized economy shifts financial power away from large corporations and into the hands of individual users, creating a system where content is valued based on quality and community support rather than corporate-driven metrics.

Several decentralized social media platforms have already gained traction as alternatives to mainstream networks. Mastodon is an open-source microblogging platform that functions similarly to Twitter but is built on a federated system, where multiple independently operated servers communicate with each other rather than relying on a single centralized database. This allows users to choose servers based on their interests, community values, or moderation preferences. Similarly, platforms like Minds and Steemit use blockchain technology to reward users with cryptocurrency for creating and curating content, offering an incentive-based system that challenges the advertising model of traditional social media. Other projects, such as Bluesky, backed by Twitter co-founder Jack Dorsey, explore new decentralized protocols that aim to reshape how social networks function at their core.

Despite their potential, decentralized social media platforms face significant challenges. One of the primary hurdles is scalability. Traditional platforms like Facebook and YouTube handle billions of users with complex content delivery systems optimized for speed and efficiency. Decentralized platforms, which rely on distributed networks and blockchain transactions, often struggle to achieve the same level of performance, leading to slower loading times, higher storage costs, and technical limitations that impact user experience. For these platforms to compete with mainstream social media, they must develop infrastructure that can support mass adoption without compromising decentralization principles.

Another challenge is content moderation. While decentralization allows for greater freedom of expression, it also raises concerns about the spread of misinformation, hate speech, and harmful content. Without centralized oversight, enforcing community standards becomes more difficult, and platforms risk becoming havens for unregulated or illegal content. Some decentralized platforms implement reputation-based moderation systems, where users earn credibility based on their contributions and behavior, influencing how content is ranked or moderated. Others rely on community-driven governance models to establish ethical guidelines. However, these approaches are still experimental, and finding a balance between free speech and responsible moderation remains an ongoing challenge.

User adoption is another factor that will determine the success of decentralized social media. Many people are accustomed to the convenience, familiarity, and network effects of mainstream platforms, making it difficult to convince them to switch to decentralized alternatives. The lack of widespread awareness, the technical learning curve, and the absence of major influencers or brands on these platforms also limit their growth. To attract more users, decentralized networks must offer intuitive interfaces, seamless onboarding experiences, and compelling incentives that make switching platforms worthwhile.

Regulatory scrutiny will also shape the future of decentralized social media. Governments around the world are increasingly focusing on digital regulation, addressing issues such as misinformation, online harassment, data privacy, and content accountability. Decentralized platforms, which operate outside the control of traditional tech companies, may face legal challenges as authorities attempt to enforce compliance with existing laws. Decentralized systems that prioritize anonymity and resistance to censorship could become targets for stricter regulations, especially in regions where governments seek greater control over digital communications.

As decentralized social media platforms continue to evolve, they have the potential to redefine the way people interact online. By shifting control away from corporations and giving users greater autonomy over their data, content, and monetization, these platforms challenge the centralized model that has dominated the internet for decades. However, the road to mainstream adoption will require overcoming technical, ethical, and regulatory hurdles. Whether decentralized social media becomes the future of digital communication or remains a niche alternative will depend on how well these platforms address these challenges while maintaining their core principles of transparency, freedom, and user empowerment.

Can We Make Ethical Algorithms?

Algorithms shape nearly every aspect of modern digital life, from determining what content appears in social media feeds to influencing financial decisions, job applications, and even healthcare recommendations. These complex systems process vast amounts of data to make automated decisions that impact millions of people daily. While algorithms have the potential to enhance efficiency, convenience, and personalization, they also introduce ethical concerns related to bias, privacy, accountability, and manipulation. The question of whether we can create truly ethical algorithms remains one of the most pressing challenges in the development of artificial intelligence and machine learning.

One of the primary ethical concerns with algorithms is bias. Despite being perceived as objective decision-making tools, algorithms reflect the data they are trained on and the choices made by their developers. If an algorithm is trained on biased data, it will inevitably produce biased results, reinforcing existing inequalities rather than eliminating them. Studies have shown that algorithms used for hiring processes, predictive policing, and loan approvals have exhibited racial and gender biases, disproportionately disadvantaging certain groups. These biases arise because historical data often reflects systemic inequalities, and if not carefully accounted for, algorithms amplify these patterns rather than correcting them.

Addressing bias in algorithms requires careful curation of training data and ongoing monitoring of decision-making processes. Developers must ensure that datasets are diverse, representative, and free from historical prejudices. However, eliminating bias entirely is nearly impossible because real-world data inherently carries social, economic, and political complexities. Even with the best intentions, defining fairness is subjective—what one group considers a fair outcome may not align with another's perspective. Ethical algorithm design requires making value-based decisions about which biases to correct and how to balance competing interests, a challenge that extends beyond technical considerations into philosophical and political debates.

Transparency is another key factor in developing ethical algorithms. Many algorithms function as black boxes, meaning that even their developers do not fully understand how they arrive at certain decisions. Machine learning models, particularly deep learning systems, operate through layers of complex calculations that make it difficult to trace how an input leads to a specific output. This lack of explainability creates serious ethical dilemmas, especially when algorithmic decisions affect people's lives in meaningful ways, such as determining access to credit, employment, or medical treatment. Without transparency, users cannot challenge unfair outcomes, and organizations cannot be held accountable for biased or harmful decisions.

To make algorithms more ethical, developers must prioritize explainability, also known as algorithmic transparency. This involves designing models that provide clear reasoning for their decisions, allowing users to understand why certain choices were made. Some researchers are exploring techniques such as interpretable AI, which simplifies complex decision-making processes into human-readable explanations. Regulatory efforts have also begun pushing for greater transparency, with laws such as the General Data Protection Regulation (GDPR) in the European Union requiring companies to explain automated decisions that affect individuals. However, achieving a balance between transparency and performance remains challenging, as more interpretable models are often less powerful than their black-box counterparts.

Privacy is another major ethical concern related to algorithmic decision-making. Many modern algorithms rely on vast amounts of user data to function effectively, analyzing personal information to refine recommendations, target advertisements, and optimize engagement. However, this level of data collection raises serious questions about consent, surveillance, and individual autonomy. Users often have little control over how their data is collected and used, and algorithmic systems can infer sensitive personal details that individuals never explicitly shared. For example, algorithms can predict political affiliations, sexual orientation, or mental health conditions based on seemingly unrelated online behavior.

To build ethical algorithms, developers must implement strict data privacy protections, ensuring that users have control over their personal information. Privacy-preserving technologies such as differential privacy and federated learning offer potential solutions by allowing algorithms to learn from data without directly accessing individual records. These techniques enable companies to maintain personalization without compromising user privacy. However, the business models of many tech companies rely on data-driven advertising, creating a conflict of interest between ethical data use and profitability. Without strong regulatory oversight, the incentive to prioritize privacy over revenue remains weak.

Another ethical challenge is the potential for algorithms to manipulate user behavior. Social media algorithms, for example, are designed to maximize engagement, often by promoting emotionally charged or addictive content. Studies have shown that outrage, fear, and sensationalism generate higher engagement, leading algorithms to prioritize divisive content that deepens political polarization and misinformation. While platforms argue that their goal is to enhance user experience, the reality is that engagement-driven algorithms optimize for profit, keeping users on the platform for as long as possible regardless of the social consequences.

Creating ethical algorithms requires shifting priorities away from engagement maximization toward well-being optimization. Some researchers suggest designing algorithms that encourage healthy interactions, promote diverse perspectives, and reduce exposure to harmful content. For example, instead of ranking content purely based on engagement metrics, platforms could integrate measures of informational quality, emotional impact, or user well-being. However, making these changes requires companies to accept potential reductions in revenue, a difficult tradeoff in a competitive industry where attention equals profit.

Accountability in algorithmic decision-making is another crucial aspect of ethical design. When an algorithm produces a harmful outcome—such as falsely flagging content, denying someone a loan, or spreading misinformation—who is responsible? In traditional decision-making, human oversight provides a mechanism for accountability, but in automated systems, responsibility often becomes diffused. Companies may blame the complexity of the algorithm, developers may point to the data, and users may feel powerless to challenge decisions.

To address this, ethical algorithms must include mechanisms for human oversight and appeals processes. Users should have the ability to contest algorithmic decisions and request human review when necessary. Governments and regulatory bodies must establish legal frameworks that hold companies accountable for algorithmic harm, ensuring that automated systems are subject to the same ethical standards as human decision-makers. Some experts advocate for algorithmic audits, where independent third parties evaluate the fairness, accuracy, and societal impact of AI systems. Such measures can help ensure that companies remain responsible for the technology they deploy.

The question of whether truly ethical algorithms can exist remains complex, as ethical considerations are often in conflict with business interests, technological limitations, and differing societal values. However, by prioritizing fairness, transparency, privacy, and accountability, developers can create algorithms that minimize harm and promote positive outcomes. Achieving ethical AI requires collaboration between technologists, policymakers, ethicists, and the public, ensuring that automated decision-making serves humanity rather than exploits it. As technology continues to evolve, the pursuit of ethical algorithms will remain one of the most important challenges in shaping the future of artificial intelligence and digital society.

Privacy Concerns in the Age of Algorithmic Social Media

Social media has become deeply embedded in daily life, offering platforms for communication, entertainment, and commerce. However, behind the convenience and connectivity lies a vast ecosystem of data collection, tracking, and surveillance, driven by algorithmic decision-making. Social media platforms rely on sophisticated algorithms to curate content, recommend posts, and personalize user experiences, but these same algorithms also pose significant privacy risks. The vast amounts of personal data collected by platforms raise concerns about surveillance, data breaches, algorithmic profiling, and the erosion of digital privacy. As social media companies continue to refine their data-driven models, users face increasing challenges in maintaining control over their personal information.

One of the primary privacy concerns in algorithmic social media is the sheer scale of data collection. Every action a user takes—likes, comments, shares, time spent on posts, search history, location data, and even biometric information—is tracked and analyzed to build detailed behavioral profiles. This data allows platforms to make predictions about user preferences, emotions, and future behaviors. While some users appreciate personalized recommendations, many remain unaware of how much data is being collected and how it is used. Social media companies justify this extensive tracking by arguing that it enhances user experience, but the reality is that most of this data is monetized through targeted advertising and sold to third-party entities.

Algorithmic profiling is another major privacy risk. Social media platforms use artificial intelligence to categorize users based on their behavior, interactions, and personal characteristics. These profiles determine the type of content shown in feeds, the advertisements displayed, and even the connections suggested. While profiling helps refine user experiences, it also raises ethical questions about consent and control. Users have little say in how they are categorized, and incorrect profiling can lead to biases that impact everything from job opportunities to financial decisions. Individuals may be placed into groups they did not choose, affecting their digital reputation and shaping their online identity in ways they cannot easily change.

Data tracking extends beyond social media platforms, following users across the internet. Many websites integrate tracking pixels, cookies, and hidden scripts that allow social media companies to monitor user activity even when they are not actively using the platform. Facebook's Pixel, Google Analytics, and other tracking technologies enable companies to collect information on browsing habits, purchases, and interactions with other websites. This cross-platform tracking creates a comprehensive digital fingerprint that companies use to refine their algorithms further. Even users who do not have social media accounts can be tracked through shadow profiles, where data about them is collected from friends, contact lists, and public sources. This level of surveillance raises concerns about whether true digital privacy is even possible in the modern internet era.

Data breaches and leaks have further highlighted the dangers of algorithmic social media's extensive data collection. Large-scale breaches have exposed millions of user records, revealing sensitive information such as passwords, messages, and private interactions. Hackers and cybercriminals can exploit these vulnerabilities, leading to identity theft, financial fraud, and reputational damage. When personal data is leaked, users often have little recourse, as once information is exposed, it is nearly impossible to erase from the internet. Social media companies frequently promise to improve security measures, but the continued occurrence of data breaches demonstrates that no system is entirely safe from exploitation.

The rise of facial recognition technology and biometric tracking in social media adds another layer of privacy risks. Platforms like Facebook, Instagram, and TikTok have experimented with facial recognition features that identify individuals in photos and videos, even without their explicit consent. While these technologies offer conveniences such as automatic tagging and enhanced security features, they also create risks of mass surveillance and misuse. Governments, advertisers, and even malicious actors can access biometric data, using it for tracking, law enforcement, or social control. Many users are unaware that their facial data is stored indefinitely, making it vulnerable to future technological developments that could repurpose it in ways never originally intended.

Privacy policies on social media platforms are often lengthy, complex, and filled with legal jargon that makes it difficult for the average user to understand what they are agreeing to. Many platforms use opt-out models, where users are automatically enrolled in data collection practices and must actively find settings to disable tracking. Even when privacy controls are available, they are often hidden behind multiple layers of menus, discouraging users from adjusting them. The lack of transparency in how data is collected, stored, and shared prevents users from making fully informed decisions about their online privacy.

Governments and regulatory bodies have begun responding to privacy concerns with legislation aimed at protecting user data. The European Union's General Data Protection Regulation (GDPR) requires companies to disclose how they collect and process personal data, granting users the right to access, delete, and control their information.

The California Consumer Privacy Act (CCPA) provides similar protections, allowing consumers to opt out of data sales and request greater transparency from tech companies. While these laws have increased awareness of digital privacy, enforcement remains a challenge, as many companies find ways to circumvent regulations or continue collecting data under different legal justifications.

Despite growing awareness of privacy risks, many users continue to engage with social media platforms without fully understanding the implications of data tracking. The convenience of personalized feeds, recommendations, and targeted advertising often outweighs concerns about surveillance. Additionally, the dominance of social media in communication, business, and entertainment makes it difficult for individuals to opt out entirely. While some privacy-conscious users employ tools like VPNs, encrypted messaging apps, and browser extensions to limit tracking, these measures require technical knowledge that many users do not possess. The digital ecosystem is designed in a way that makes full privacy protection difficult, reinforcing the trade-off between usability and security.

The future of privacy in algorithmic social media depends on how companies, governments, and users address these concerns. Tech companies face increasing pressure to implement privacy-focused features, such as end-to-end encryption, anonymous browsing options, and more transparent data policies. Some platforms have introduced limited privacy controls, such as Apple's App Tracking Transparency feature, which allows users to prevent apps from tracking their activity across different websites and apps. However, these measures often conflict with the advertising-driven business models of social media companies, which rely on data collection to maximize revenue.

As artificial intelligence and machine learning continue to advance, the potential for even deeper surveillance and algorithmic profiling increases. Emerging technologies such as predictive behavior modeling, neural interfaces, and biometric authentication could further blur the lines between convenience and privacy invasion. Users will need to remain vigilant, demanding greater transparency and stronger legal protections to safeguard their personal information. Social media platforms must take responsibility for developing ethical data practices that prioritize user control over corporate profit. Privacy in the age of algorithmic social media is not just a technical issue but a fundamental question about how digital society should be structured and who has the right to control personal information in an increasingly interconnected world.

How AI-Powered Algorithms Shape Trends

Social media has become the primary driver of global trends, influencing everything from fashion and music to politics and consumer behavior. Behind this trend-setting power are AI-powered algorithms that determine which content gets amplified and which remains unseen. These algorithms are not just passive systems that reflect public interest; they actively shape what becomes popular by prioritizing certain types of content, boosting engagement-driven posts, and adapting to user preferences in real time. The influence of AI on trends is so profound that entire industries now rely on algorithmic visibility to succeed, making social media platforms not just digital spaces for interaction but powerful cultural and economic forces.

AI-driven recommendation systems play a crucial role in trend formation by curating personalized feeds based on user behavior. Platforms like TikTok, Instagram, YouTube, and Twitter analyze millions of interactions every second, identifying patterns in likes, shares, watch time, and engagement metrics. These systems detect emerging interests and push specific content to more users, accelerating the viral spread of trends. The more users engage with a particular post, the more the algorithm promotes it, creating a feedback loop where content gains momentum rapidly. This process enables trends to form almost instantaneously, often with little to no involvement from traditional media or marketing campaigns.

One of the most significant ways AI-powered algorithms shape trends is through the amplification of viral challenges. TikTok, in particular, has mastered this process, with its For You Page algorithm detecting and promoting content that resonates with users. Dance trends, meme formats, and challenges can emerge from a single video, spreading across millions of accounts in a matter of days. Unlike traditional trends that relied on celebrity endorsements or media exposure, AI-driven trends originate from ordinary users who happen to create content that aligns with algorithmic preferences. Once a trend gains traction, creators rush to participate, reinforcing its popularity and making it a defining cultural moment.

Music trends have also been deeply influenced by AI algorithms. Streaming services and social media platforms analyze listening habits to recommend songs, but they also play an active role in pushing specific tracks. TikTok's AI, for example, identifies songs with high engagement potential and boosts videos that use them, turning previously unknown tracks into chart-topping hits. Musicians and record labels now strategize around this system, crafting songs that fit TikTok's viral formula—short, catchy, and easily remixable. This shift has altered the music industry, making social media algorithms a determining factor in which artists succeed and which songs dominate streaming charts.

Fashion and consumer trends follow a similar pattern, with algorithms identifying rising styles and amplifying influencers who promote them. Instagram and Pinterest use AI to analyze images and detect trending aesthetics, guiding brands on what products to highlight. Fast fashion companies leverage these insights to rapidly produce clothing that aligns with social media trends, shortening the traditional fashion cycle from months to weeks. Consumers are exposed to curated product recommendations based on their browsing history, reinforcing purchasing behaviors that align with emerging styles. The influence of AI-powered trend detection has led to the rise of micro-trends, where specific aesthetics gain popularity for short bursts before being replaced by the next algorithmically promoted wave.

Political and social trends are also shaped by AI algorithms, often with significant real-world consequences. Platforms prioritize content that generates engagement, which often means amplifying emotionally charged posts. Outrage, activism, and polarizing discussions tend to receive high levels of interaction, prompting AI systems to push them into more feeds. This has led to the rapid spread of political movements, viral social justice campaigns, and online debates that shape public opinion. While this amplification can be a force for positive change, such as mobilizing support for humanitarian causes, it can also contribute to misinformation and ideological echo chambers. AI does not differentiate between constructive discourse and divisive rhetoric; it simply prioritizes what keeps users engaged the longest.

The way AI-powered algorithms shape trends has also created challenges for brands and influencers trying to maintain relevance. The unpredictability of algorithmic changes means that what worked yesterday may not work tomorrow. Content creators must constantly adapt, experimenting with new formats, posting strategies, and engagement tactics to remain visible. Many influencers and businesses now rely on data analytics tools to decode algorithmic patterns, attempting to reverse-engineer what will be prioritized next. This reliance on AI-driven trends has made social media a highly competitive space, where success is dictated not just by creativity but by an understanding of the platform's evolving algorithms.

The increasing role of AI in trend formation has also led to concerns about authenticity and manipulation. Because algorithms favor engagement, some users exploit this by creating content specifically designed to trigger emotional responses. Sensationalized posts, exaggerated reactions, and clickbait-style videos perform well because they align with AI's preference for content that maximizes interaction. This has led to the rise of manufactured trends, where brands or influencers deliberately engineer viral moments to gain visibility. While organic trends still emerge, the ability to manipulate AI-driven amplification has blurred the lines between genuine cultural movements and artificially boosted content.

Another ethical concern is the reinforcement of biases within AI-driven trend formation. Algorithms learn from user behavior, which means they can unintentionally perpetuate existing societal biases. If certain types of content historically receive more engagement, AI systems will continue to prioritize them, potentially sidelining underrepresented voices. This dynamic has been observed in cases where algorithmic biases favor certain body types, racial backgrounds, or content styles, limiting the diversity of trends that gain mainstream visibility. Social media companies have begun addressing these issues by adjusting their algorithms, but bias remains an inherent challenge in machine learning models that rely on past data to predict future trends.

As AI-powered algorithms continue to evolve, their influence over trend formation will only grow stronger. Future developments in artificial intelligence, such as real-time predictive modeling and generative AI, could further refine how trends are detected and promoted. Personalized trend curation may become even more sophisticated, where each user experiences a unique, AI-generated digital culture tailored specifically to their preferences. While this level of customization could enhance user experience, it also raises questions about whether shared cultural moments will become less common, as trends become increasingly fragmented across algorithmically determined micro-communities.

The dominance of AI in shaping trends highlights the power social media platforms hold in defining culture, commerce, and public discourse. While algorithms have democratized trend creation, allowing ordinary users to influence global movements, they have also concentrated power in the hands of tech companies that control these systems. As platforms continue refining their algorithms, the challenge will be ensuring that trend formation remains authentic, diverse, and ethical. Users, creators, and businesses must navigate a digital landscape where AI is not just a passive tool but an active force shaping what people see, engage with, and ultimately consider important in society.

The Battle Against Algorithmic Manipulation

As social media algorithms continue to dictate content visibility, engagement, and influence, they have become prime targets for manipulation. Algorithmic manipulation refers to the strategic exploitation of social media ranking systems to amplify certain content, distort public perception, and achieve artificial popularity. Governments, businesses, influencers, and malicious actors all seek ways to game these systems to serve their interests, leading to a digital landscape where authenticity is increasingly difficult to distinguish from manipulation. The battle against algorithmic manipulation has become a pressing issue for platforms, regulators, and users alike, as unchecked exploitation of algorithms threatens the integrity of online discourse, public trust, and democratic processes.

One of the most common forms of algorithmic manipulation is the use of bots and automated engagement tactics. Social media bots are programmed accounts that mimic human behavior, artificially inflating likes, shares, comments, and follower counts. These bots can be used to push specific narratives, manipulate public opinion, or create the illusion of widespread support for a particular idea. Political campaigns, corporate marketing teams, and propagandists have all leveraged bot networks to amplify content beyond its organic reach, tricking social media algorithms into believing that certain topics are more popular or legitimate than they actually are.

Click farms and engagement rings represent another form of algorithmic manipulation, where individuals or groups coordinate to artificially boost content visibility. Click farms consist of low-wage workers paid to interact with posts, simulating real engagement to deceive algorithms. Engagement rings operate on a more grassroots level, with groups of users agreeing to like, comment, and share each other's content to trigger algorithmic promotion. While these methods are often used by influencers, small businesses, and activists trying to gain traction, they distort the natural content ranking system, making it difficult for genuinely engaging or high-quality content to rise to the top without artificial boosts.

Another major threat posed by algorithmic manipulation is the deliberate spread of misinformation and fake news. False or misleading content is often engineered to exploit algorithmic preferences for emotionally charged, high-engagement material. Sensationalist headlines, conspiracy theories, and divisive political content generate strong reactions, leading social media algorithms to prioritize their distribution. Malicious actors use manipulation tactics to spread misinformation rapidly, taking advantage of the fact that fact-checking and moderation systems often struggle to keep pace with viral falsehoods. The consequences of algorithmic manipulation in this form are significant, as misinformation can sway public opinion, influence elections, and contribute to societal polarization.

Deepfake technology and AI-generated content add another layer to the challenges of combating algorithmic manipulation. Deepfakes use artificial intelligence to create hyper-realistic videos and images that can depict people saying or doing things they never actually did. When combined with algorithmic exploitation, deepfake content can be strategically released to deceive audiences and manipulate public perception. Similarly, AI-generated text and social media posts can flood platforms with content designed to mimic real conversations, making it increasingly difficult for users to identify authentic interactions. As these technologies become more sophisticated, distinguishing between real and manipulated content will become an even greater challenge.

Platforms have responded to algorithmic manipulation with a range of countermeasures, but these efforts have proven to be an ongoing arms race. One of the primary strategies involves improving bot detection and removal systems. Advanced AI models analyze user behavior patterns to identify inauthentic accounts, flagging them for deletion. However, bot creators continuously refine their methods, designing accounts that behave more like real users to evade detection. Despite efforts to purge fake accounts, bot networks continue to evolve, adapting to new algorithmic defenses as platforms struggle to keep up.

Fact-checking and content moderation initiatives also play a role in combating manipulation, but they come with their own set of challenges. Many platforms partner with independent fact-checkers to verify claims and flag misinformation, reducing the visibility of misleading content. However, these efforts are often met with resistance, as users may perceive fact-checking as biased or politically motivated. Additionally, moderation at scale is an immense challenge, as human review teams cannot keep up with the volume of content being produced. AI moderation tools, while useful, still struggle with nuance, context, and rapidly evolving manipulation tactics.

Algorithmic transparency is another approach that platforms are exploring to counter manipulation. By making ranking and recommendation criteria more visible, users can better understand why certain content appears in their feeds. Transparency can help expose manipulation tactics, allowing users to make more informed decisions about the content they engage with. Some platforms have introduced tools that let users see why a post was recommended or allow them to adjust their algorithmic preferences. However, full transparency is difficult to achieve, as social media companies are reluctant to disclose too much information about their algorithms for fear of further exploitation.

Regulatory efforts to combat algorithmic manipulation are also gaining traction. Governments and policymakers have begun introducing laws that hold platforms accountable for the spread of manipulated content, requiring them to implement stricter measures against misinformation, bot activity, and deceptive advertising. Some countries have enacted regulations requiring platforms to label AI-generated content or remove harmful disinformation campaigns. However, regulation is a double-edged sword, as overly broad policies can risk infringing on free speech and legitimate activism. Striking a balance between combating manipulation and protecting digital rights remains a complex challenge.

Users themselves play a role in the fight against algorithmic manipulation. Digital literacy and critical thinking skills are essential tools for recognizing manipulated content and avoiding engagement with deceptive tactics. Many organizations and educators are working to improve public awareness of misinformation, teaching users how to identify bots, verify sources, and critically analyze online narratives. However, the sheer volume of content on social media makes it difficult for individual users to independently fact-check every piece of information they encounter. This reality underscores the need for systemic solutions that address manipulation at its root rather than relying solely on individual responsibility.

Despite efforts to combat algorithmic manipulation, the problem persists, largely because platforms are designed to prioritize engagement and profitability. Social media companies benefit from high levels of user activity, which means that content that generates strong reactions—whether real or manipulated—often remains highly visible. Until platforms fundamentally shift their ranking systems to prioritize informational integrity over engagement metrics, algorithmic manipulation will continue to be an issue. Ethical AI design, improved moderation tools, and a commitment to transparency will be essential in shaping a digital ecosystem that resists manipulation while preserving the open exchange of ideas.

As artificial intelligence and social media algorithms become more sophisticated, the battle against algorithmic manipulation will only intensify. Manipulative tactics will evolve, and platforms will need to continuously adapt their defenses. The fight for authenticity in the digital world is an ongoing struggle, requiring cooperation between tech companies, policymakers, educators, and users. The outcome of this battle will determine whether social media remains a tool for genuine connection and discourse or continues to be a battleground where manipulation dictates reality.

The Relationship Between Algorithms and User Behavior

Social media algorithms shape the way people interact with digital content, influencing what they see, how they engage, and even how they think. These complex systems do not just passively respond to user behavior; they actively mold it, creating feedback loops that reinforce certain habits, interests, and emotional responses. The relationship between algorithms and user behavior is a dynamic one, where users influence algorithms through their actions, while algorithms, in turn, condition users to behave in specific ways. This interaction has profound implications for attention, decision-making, and even mental health, as platforms continuously refine their models to maximize engagement and user retention.

One of the most significant ways algorithms affect user behavior is by determining the visibility of content. Social media platforms analyze countless data points to decide which posts, videos, and advertisements should be prioritized in a user's feed. These ranking systems are designed to keep people on the platform for as long as possible, showing them content that aligns with their past interactions. If a user frequently watches videos related to a particular topic, the algorithm will push more similar content, reinforcing their interests and guiding their future behavior. This process creates a self-reinforcing loop, where users become increasingly immersed in specific types of content, sometimes without realizing how their preferences are being shaped by algorithmic recommendations.

The way users engage with content also teaches algorithms how to refine their predictions. Every like, comment, share, and pause is recorded and analyzed to fine-tune content recommendations. Algorithms learn to predict which posts are likely to generate reactions, and they prioritize those that provoke strong emotions. Studies have shown that content that elicits anger, outrage, or excitement tends to perform better because it encourages interaction. As a result, algorithms often amplify emotionally charged content, influencing how users perceive and react to information. This mechanism can drive social polarization, as users are consistently exposed to content that reinforces their existing beliefs and emotions, making them more likely to engage with extreme or divisive material.

The influence of algorithms extends beyond content consumption to shaping how users interact with others. The design of social media platforms encourages behaviors that align with algorithmic priorities. For example, features like infinite scrolling, autoplay, and notification systems are engineered to keep users engaged. The more time users spend on a platform, the more data algorithms can collect, refining their ability to predict and influence behavior. This cycle creates habits where users check their feeds compulsively, even when they had no intention of doing so. The addictive nature of algorithm-driven platforms has led to concerns about attention spans, productivity, and overall mental well-being.

Algorithms also influence decision-making by controlling the flow of information. In an era where people rely on social media for news, entertainment, and education, algorithms play a crucial role in shaping public knowledge. Search engines and recommendation systems prioritize certain sources over others, influencing what users perceive as credible or important. This can lead to filter bubbles, where individuals are only exposed to viewpoints that align with their existing beliefs. Over time, this effect can create ideological echo chambers, where users become less likely to encounter diverse perspectives, reinforcing biases and limiting critical thinking.

Personalized content feeds have further blurred the line between genuine preferences and algorithmically driven behavior. Many users believe they are making independent choices about what to watch, read, or purchase, when in reality, their options have already been curated by an algorithm. Online shopping platforms use AI-driven recommendations to guide purchasing decisions, while music and video streaming services introduce users to content that aligns with previous listening and viewing habits. The illusion of choice creates a sense of autonomy, but the reality is that algorithms play an active role in shaping tastes, trends, and consumption patterns.

Social validation mechanisms, such as likes, shares, and comments, further reinforce algorithmic influence on behavior. When a post gains traction, algorithms push it to more users, creating a snowball effect. This dynamic encourages people to create content that aligns with algorithmic preferences, prioritizing engagement over authenticity. Influencers, businesses, and content creators often adjust their strategies based on what algorithms favor, leading to the homogenization of content. Over time, originality may take a backseat to what is most likely to succeed within an algorithmic framework, creating digital environments that prioritize trends and virality over depth and nuance.

The psychological impact of algorithm-driven content delivery is an area of growing concern. Social media algorithms are optimized to keep users engaged, but they do not necessarily prioritize well-being. Studies have linked excessive social media use to anxiety, depression, and reduced self-esteem, particularly among younger users. The curated nature of algorithmic feeds can create unrealistic expectations about life, success, and beauty, as users are frequently exposed to idealized versions of reality. Additionally, algorithms that prioritize sensational or negative news can contribute to heightened stress and feelings of helplessness, as users are repeatedly exposed to distressing information.

Despite these concerns, algorithms are not inherently negative. When used responsibly, they can enhance digital experiences by providing users with relevant and meaningful content. Personalized learning platforms use AI-driven recommendations to help students improve their skills, while health-focused algorithms can suggest fitness routines or mental wellness strategies. The key challenge is ensuring that algorithms serve users' best interests rather than purely maximizing engagement for corporate profit. Ethical AI design, transparency, and user empowerment are essential for creating systems that enhance well-being while respecting personal agency.

As artificial intelligence continues to evolve, the relationship between algorithms and user behavior will become even more complex. Future advancements in machine learning will enable even more precise behavioral predictions, raising questions about how much control individuals truly have over their digital experiences. The challenge for social media companies, policymakers, and users alike is to find ways to balance personalization with ethical considerations, ensuring that algorithms support healthy and informed interactions rather than exploiting human psychology for engagement. Recognizing the ways in which algorithms shape behavior is the first step in creating a more transparent and responsible digital ecosystem where users maintain agency over their online experiences.

The Role of Governments in Regulating Algorithms

As artificial intelligence and machine learning play an increasingly central role in shaping digital interactions, governments around the world are grappling with the challenge of regulating algorithms. These systems influence everything from social media feeds and search results to financial decisions and law enforcement, raising significant concerns about privacy, bias, misinformation, and corporate power. While algorithms drive innovation and efficiency, they also pose risks when left unchecked. Governments have begun to introduce regulations to ensure transparency, accountability, and fairness in algorithmic decision-making, but balancing regulation with technological progress remains a complex and evolving challenge.

One of the primary reasons for government intervention in algorithmic regulation is the issue of transparency. Many algorithms operate as black boxes, meaning that their decision-making processes are not publicly disclosed or easily understood, even by their own developers. This opacity makes it difficult for users to know why certain content is promoted, why some job applications are rejected, or why loan approvals are denied. Governments have pushed for greater transparency in algorithmic systems, requiring companies to disclose how their algorithms function and what data they use. Regulations such as the European Union's General Data Protection Regulation (GDPR) mandate that companies provide explanations for automated decisions that affect individuals, allowing users to challenge unfair outcomes.

Bias and discrimination are also key concerns driving government regulation of algorithms. Machine learning models are trained on historical data, which can reflect societal biases. If an algorithm is used in hiring, policing, or lending, and it is trained on biased data, it may produce discriminatory outcomes that disproportionately impact certain groups. Governments have introduced laws that require companies to audit their algorithms for bias, ensuring that automated systems do not reinforce existing inequalities. Some jurisdictions are considering mandatory fairness assessments for AI-driven decisions, requiring companies to test for discriminatory patterns before deploying their models.

Misinformation and online manipulation are additional areas where governments are stepping in to regulate algorithms. Social media platforms use algorithms to prioritize content that maximizes engagement, often amplifying sensational, misleading, or divisive information. Governments have proposed regulations requiring platforms to take greater responsibility for the content that their algorithms promote. Some countries have introduced laws that hold tech companies accountable for the spread of false information, requiring them to remove harmful content or apply warning labels to manipulated media. While these efforts aim to combat misinformation, they also raise concerns about censorship and the potential for governments to use algorithmic regulation as a tool for controlling political discourse.

Privacy protection is another major focus of algorithmic regulation. Many platforms collect vast amounts of user data to refine their recommendation systems and advertising models. Governments have introduced data protection laws that limit how much information companies can collect, how long they can store it, and how it can be used. Regulations such as the California Consumer Privacy Act (CCPA) give users the right to know what data is being collected about them and to opt out of certain tracking practices. In some cases, governments have imposed restrictions on cross-border data transfers, requiring companies to store user data within specific jurisdictions to prevent foreign access to sensitive information.

The role of governments in regulating algorithms extends beyond content moderation and data privacy to areas such as economic competition. Tech companies that develop and control major algorithms wield immense market power, often shaping entire industries. Search engines, e-commerce platforms, and social media giants can influence consumer behavior, giving preferential treatment to their own services while sidelining competitors. Governments have launched antitrust investigations into major tech companies to determine whether their algorithmic practices create unfair market advantages. Some regulators have proposed measures that require platforms to provide greater visibility to smaller businesses and third-party developers, preventing monopolistic control over digital ecosystems.

Regulating artificial intelligence and algorithmic decision-making in law enforcement and the criminal justice system is another critical issue. Predictive policing algorithms analyze historical crime data to determine where law enforcement resources should be allocated. While these systems aim to improve efficiency, they have been criticized for disproportionately targeting marginalized communities, reinforcing existing biases in policing. Facial recognition technology, often powered by AI algorithms, has also come under scrutiny for its inaccuracies, particularly in identifying people of color. Some governments have banned the use of facial recognition for surveillance purposes, while others have introduced stricter guidelines for its deployment in law enforcement.

The financial sector is another area where government regulation of algorithms is becoming increasingly important. AI-driven algorithms are used to assess creditworthiness, detect fraudulent transactions, and automate investment strategies. While these systems improve efficiency and reduce human bias, they also introduce risks such as algorithmic trading errors and discriminatory lending practices. Governments have implemented regulations requiring financial institutions to ensure fairness and transparency in their automated decision-making processes. Some jurisdictions have mandated that individuals have the right to appeal algorithmic financial decisions, ensuring that humans remain in the loop when major financial determinations are made.

The challenge of regulating algorithms is that technology evolves faster than legal frameworks. Many governments struggle to keep pace with the rapid development of AI and machine learning, leading to regulatory gaps that companies exploit. Some policymakers advocate for agile regulation—an approach that allows for continuous updates and adaptations to laws as technology advances. Others propose independent oversight bodies that specialize in algorithmic accountability, providing expert analysis and recommendations for policy changes. These regulatory approaches aim to strike a balance between protecting users and fostering technological innovation.

Global coordination is another obstacle in algorithmic regulation. While some countries have introduced strict AI laws, others take a more lenient approach, creating inconsistencies in how algorithms are governed across borders. International organizations and regulatory alliances have started working toward common standards for AI and algorithmic decision-making, promoting ethical guidelines that companies can follow regardless of jurisdiction. However, enforcing these standards remains difficult, as different governments have varying perspectives on issues such as data privacy, free speech, and corporate regulation.

The debate over how much governments should intervene in algorithmic decision-making is ongoing. Some argue that excessive regulation stifles innovation, making it harder for tech companies to develop new technologies that benefit society. Others believe that without strong oversight, algorithms will continue to perpetuate harm, reinforcing inequalities, spreading misinformation, and exploiting user data. Governments must navigate these competing interests, ensuring that regulation protects individuals while allowing for technological advancement.

As artificial intelligence continues to shape the digital landscape, the role of governments in regulating algorithms will become even more critical. Policymakers must balance the need for transparency, fairness, and privacy with the realities of global competition and technological progress. By developing adaptable, enforceable, and internationally aligned regulatory frameworks, governments can help ensure that algorithms serve the public good rather than corporate or political interests. The future of algorithmic regulation will depend on how effectively governments, tech companies, and civil society collaborate to create systems that prioritize accountability while fostering responsible innovation.

Algorithm Transparency: What We Know and What We Don't

Algorithms power nearly every aspect of the digital world, from social media feeds and search engine results to financial services and healthcare decisions. They determine what information is surfaced, what content is prioritized, and how individuals interact with digital platforms. Despite their immense influence, these algorithms largely operate in the shadows, with little insight into how they make decisions. Algorithm transparency—the idea that users, researchers, and policymakers should have access to information about how algorithms function—has become a growing demand as concerns about bias, misinformation, and digital manipulation increase. While some platforms have taken steps to provide more visibility into their decision-making processes, much of the way algorithms operate remains hidden, leaving critical questions unanswered.

One of the primary reasons why algorithm transparency is difficult to achieve is the complexity of modern machine learning systems. Many of the algorithms that power social media recommendations, content moderation, and personalized advertising are built using deep learning techniques that evolve over time. These systems process vast amounts of data, adjusting their decision-making models dynamically based on user interactions. Unlike traditional rule-based systems, where inputs and outputs are predictable, deep learning algorithms often function as black boxes, meaning even their own developers cannot fully explain why a particular decision was made. This lack of interpretability raises concerns about accountability, as it becomes difficult to determine whether an algorithmic outcome was fair, biased, or flawed.

What is known about how algorithms work typically comes from company disclosures, regulatory investigations, and independent research. Some platforms have published general explanations of how their ranking systems operate. For example, YouTube has revealed that its recommendation algorithm prioritizes watch time, engagement, and user preferences to determine which videos appear in a user's feed. Similarly, Instagram has explained that its feed ranking system is influenced by factors such as content relevance, user interactions, and time spent viewing posts. However, these explanations are often vague, providing only a high-level overview rather than detailed insights into the weighting of different factors or how decisions are made in real-time.

Some transparency efforts have come through leaked internal documents and whistleblower testimonies. Former employees of major tech companies have revealed details about how algorithms are optimized for engagement, sometimes at the expense of user well-being. Reports have exposed how algorithms may amplify divisive content, prioritize emotionally charged material, and downrank content that does not drive high levels of interaction. These revelations have raised ethical concerns about whether platforms prioritize corporate profit over responsible content distribution. The lack of algorithmic transparency makes it difficult for users to know whether they are engaging with content organically or being subtly manipulated by unseen ranking mechanisms.

Despite the limited information available, certain patterns in algorithmic behavior have been identified. Social media algorithms tend to favor content that keeps users on the platform longer, rewarding posts with high engagement metrics such as likes, comments, and shares. This engagement-driven approach has been linked to the spread of misinformation, as sensationalized or emotionally charged content often generates more interactions than factual or nuanced discussions. Search engine algorithms, on the other hand, are optimized for relevance and authority, but they are still influenced by commercial interests. Paid search results, search engine optimization (SEO) strategies, and algorithmic bias can all affect what information is presented to users.

While some companies argue that full transparency is not feasible due to proprietary concerns, critics argue that opacity benefits platforms more than users. Companies protect their algorithms as trade secrets, claiming that disclosing too much information would allow bad actors to game the system. While this concern is valid—spammers, fraudsters, and misinformation peddlers could exploit transparent ranking criteria—it also allows companies to avoid scrutiny over potentially harmful algorithmic decisions. Striking a balance between protecting proprietary technology and ensuring public accountability remains one of the most significant challenges in the push for algorithmic transparency.

Regulatory efforts have attempted to bridge the transparency gap by requiring platforms to provide more insight into their algorithms. The European Union's Digital Services Act (DSA) and the General Data Protection Regulation (GDPR) include provisions for algorithmic accountability, requiring companies to explain how automated decisions impact users and provide mechanisms for appeal. Some regulators have proposed third-party audits of major algorithms, allowing independent experts to assess whether systems are fair, non-discriminatory, and in compliance with legal standards. While these measures mark progress, enforcement remains difficult, as companies often resist full disclosure or provide only partial compliance with transparency requirements.

Independent researchers have also played a crucial role in uncovering algorithmic behavior. Studies analyzing social media engagement patterns, content visibility, and recommendation biases have shed light on how platforms prioritize different types of content. However, researchers often face obstacles in accessing data, as many platforms restrict the ability to collect and analyze large-scale user interactions.

Some social media companies have shut down tools that allow researchers to track algorithmic behavior, citing privacy concerns, but critics argue that these actions hinder transparency efforts. Without access to data, it becomes challenging to hold platforms accountable for algorithmic decisions that may impact society at large.

One of the ongoing debates in the push for transparency is whether users should have more control over how algorithms function. Some platforms have introduced options to switch from algorithmically curated feeds to chronological timelines, allowing users to view content in the order it was posted rather than based on engagement-driven rankings. However, algorithmic feeds remain the default on most platforms, as they generate more user activity and, consequently, more advertising revenue. Some have suggested that users should be able to customize their own algorithms, selecting what factors they want prioritized in their content recommendations. While this idea is promising, implementing it at scale would require significant changes to platform infrastructure.

The future of algorithm transparency will likely be shaped by increasing regulatory pressure, technological advancements, and public demand. Governments are expected to introduce stricter rules requiring companies to disclose more about their algorithms, while advocacy groups and researchers will continue pushing for greater access to data. Advances in explainable AI (XAI) may also play a role in improving transparency, as new techniques are being developed to make machine learning models more interpretable. These innovations could help bridge the gap between algorithmic complexity and user understanding, allowing for more responsible and accountable AI systems.

While there is still much that remains unknown about how algorithms function, growing awareness of their impact has fueled momentum for change. Platforms may resist full transparency, but public and regulatory pressure will likely force them to be more open about how their systems operate. Understanding the relationship between algorithms and digital experiences is essential for ensuring that technology serves users rather than exploiting them. The push for transparency is not just about revealing how content is ranked—it is about ensuring that algorithms operate in ways that align with ethical principles, user interests, and societal well-being.

The Rise of Decentralized Social Media Platforms

The dominance of centralized social media platforms has sparked growing concerns about data privacy, content moderation, algorithmic bias, and corporate control over digital communication. Traditional social media giants such as Facebook, Twitter, and Instagram operate on centralized models where a single company controls user data, content distribution, and platform policies. These companies determine what users see, how content is ranked, and who can participate in discussions. As a response to these concerns, decentralized social media platforms have emerged as an alternative, offering users greater control over their data, content, and online interactions.

Decentralized social media platforms operate on blockchain technology, peer-to-peer networks, or federated models, removing the need for a central governing authority. Instead of relying on a single company to manage and regulate content, decentralized platforms distribute power among users and independent servers. This structure aims to create a more open and democratic digital space where censorship, surveillance, and algorithmic manipulation are less prevalent. By decentralizing control, these platforms provide an alternative to the walled gardens of mainstream social media, allowing for greater transparency and user autonomy.

One of the driving forces behind the rise of decentralized platforms is the increasing concern over data privacy. Centralized platforms collect vast amounts of personal data, tracking user behavior, preferences, and interactions to refine targeted advertising and algorithmic recommendations. Users often have little control over how their data is used, and high-profile data breaches have exposed vulnerabilities in centralized systems. Decentralized social media offers an alternative where data ownership remains in the hands of users. Some blockchain-based platforms use encryption and decentralized identity systems to ensure that personal information is not stored or exploited by a single entity. This shift challenges the traditional ad-driven business model of social media and prioritizes user privacy over corporate interests.

Censorship and content moderation have also played a significant role in the rise of decentralized alternatives. Centralized platforms enforce strict content policies, often removing posts, shadowbanning accounts, or deplatforming users who violate their guidelines. While content moderation is necessary to prevent the spread of harmful material, many critics argue that centralized moderation lacks transparency and disproportionately targets certain viewpoints. Decentralized platforms offer different approaches to moderation, often allowing individual communities or server administrators to set their own rules. Some platforms use decentralized autonomous organizations (DAOs) where governance decisions, including content moderation policies, are voted on by users rather than dictated by a single corporation.

Monetization models in decentralized social media differ significantly from those of traditional platforms. Most mainstream social media networks rely on advertising revenue, optimizing algorithms to maximize engagement and ad impressions. This leads to the prioritization of viral, emotionally charged, and sometimes misleading content, as engagement metrics drive platform profitability. Decentralized platforms introduce alternative monetization strategies, such as token-based economies, where users can earn cryptocurrency rewards for contributing content, curating discussions, or participating in governance. This model shifts economic power away from corporations and into the hands of individual creators and communities. Some decentralized platforms also allow users to tip content creators directly, removing intermediaries and enabling more sustainable funding models for digital content.

Several decentralized social media platforms have gained traction in response to these concerns. Mastodon, an open-source microblogging platform, operates on a federated model where different independently operated servers, known as instances, communicate with each other rather than relying on a single central authority. Users can choose which instance to join based on their preferred community values and moderation policies. Minds is another decentralized platform that incorporates blockchain technology, allowing users to earn tokens for engagement and participation. Steemit, a blockchain-based blogging platform, rewards users with cryptocurrency based on content popularity and community voting. Bluesky, an initiative supported by Twitter co-founder Jack Dorsey, is developing a decentralized protocol aimed at restructuring how social media networks operate.

Despite their potential, decentralized social media platforms face several challenges that could hinder widespread adoption. One of the primary obstacles is scalability. Centralized platforms have the infrastructure and resources to support billions of users, delivering high-speed performance and reliable services. Decentralized networks, which distribute data and processing power across multiple nodes, often struggle with slow performance, higher operational costs, and technical complexities that limit their ability to compete with mainstream platforms. Blockchain-based platforms, in particular, face scalability issues due to transaction speeds and network congestion, making it difficult to achieve the seamless experience that users expect.

User experience is another challenge for decentralized platforms. Most people are accustomed to the polished interfaces and intuitive features of mainstream social media. In contrast, many decentralized platforms require a steeper learning curve, involving concepts such as cryptocurrency wallets, private keys, and self-hosted servers. To attract a broader audience, decentralized platforms must simplify their user experience while maintaining their core principles of decentralization and user control. Without mass adoption, these platforms may remain niche alternatives rather than viable replacements for mainstream social media.

Security and moderation concerns also pose challenges for decentralized networks. While decentralization reduces the risk of corporate surveillance and censorship, it also limits the ability to combat harmful content such as misinformation, hate speech, and illegal activities. In centralized platforms, moderation teams and AI-driven detection systems can quickly identify and remove problematic content. Decentralized platforms, which rely on community-driven moderation, may struggle to enforce consistent content guidelines. Some critics argue that without effective moderation mechanisms, decentralized networks risk becoming unregulated spaces where harmful content can spread unchecked.

Regulatory scrutiny is another factor that could impact the growth of decentralized social media. Governments around the world are increasing their focus on digital regulation, addressing issues such as data privacy, misinformation, and online safety. Decentralized platforms, which operate without a central authority, pose unique regulatory challenges. Some governments may seek to impose stricter laws on decentralized networks, requiring compliance with content moderation standards, data protection regulations, and financial transparency rules for token-based economies. The decentralized nature of these platforms makes enforcement difficult, raising questions about how they will navigate legal obligations while maintaining their core principles of user autonomy and censorship resistance.

Despite these challenges, the rise of decentralized social media reflects a growing demand for alternatives that prioritize user control, privacy, and transparency. As concerns over data exploitation, censorship, and algorithmic manipulation continue to mount, decentralized networks offer a vision of social media that is less reliant on corporate interests and more aligned with democratic values. While these platforms are still in the early stages of development, continued innovation in blockchain technology, peer-to-peer networking, and decentralized governance models could pave the way for a new era of digital communication.

Whether decentralized social media can replace mainstream platforms or remain a niche alternative will depend on its ability to overcome technical and regulatory challenges while maintaining the advantages that make it appealing. The evolution of decentralized networks will shape the future of digital interactions, raising fundamental questions about who should control online spaces, how content should be moderated, and what role technology should play in shaping public discourse. As the internet continues to evolve, decentralized platforms may offer a glimpse into a future where social media is more transparent, user-driven, and resistant to centralized control.

Can We Make Ethical Algorithms?

Algorithms shape nearly every aspect of modern life, from determining what content appears on social media feeds to influencing loan approvals, hiring decisions, healthcare diagnoses, and even law enforcement practices. These automated systems are designed to process vast amounts of data efficiently, but their growing influence has raised serious ethical concerns. Bias, discrimination, privacy violations, lack of transparency, and the potential for manipulation are all issues that have emerged as algorithms become more embedded in society. The question of whether we can create truly ethical algorithms is complex, requiring a careful balance between technological innovation, fairness, accountability, and human oversight.

One of the most significant challenges in designing ethical algorithms is the issue of bias. While algorithms are often seen as neutral mathematical systems, they are built and trained on data that reflects real-world inequalities. Machine learning models learn from historical data, meaning that any biases present in that data will be perpetuated and potentially amplified by the algorithm. In hiring algorithms, for example, if past hiring practices favored certain demographics over others, the algorithm may learn to prioritize similar candidates, reinforcing existing discrimination. Facial recognition systems have been found to have higher error rates for people with darker skin tones due to biased training data. These examples highlight the ethical risks of deploying AI systems without careful evaluation of their underlying biases.

To mitigate bias, developers must carefully curate training datasets, ensuring they are diverse and representative of different populations. Bias detection tools can be used to identify and correct discriminatory patterns before an algorithm is deployed. However, even with the best efforts, completely eliminating bias is nearly impossible because fairness is not a universally agreed-upon concept. Different stakeholders may have conflicting views on what constitutes a fair outcome, making it difficult to design an algorithm that satisfies all perspectives. Ethical AI development requires continuous monitoring and adjustments to ensure that algorithms do not unintentionally cause harm or reinforce systemic inequalities.

Transparency is another critical factor in ethical algorithm design. Many AI systems operate as black boxes, meaning that their decision-making processes are opaque and difficult to interpret, even for their creators. Users affected by algorithmic decisions—such as individuals denied a loan or disqualified from a job application—often have no insight into why the decision was made. This lack of transparency raises accountability concerns, as it becomes challenging to identify and correct errors or biases.

Explainable AI (XAI) is a growing field aimed at making algorithms more interpretable and understandable to humans. By designing models that provide clear justifications for their decisions, AI systems can become more accountable and trustworthy. Regulatory measures, such as the European Union's General Data Protection Regulation (GDPR), have also begun requiring companies to provide explanations for automated decisions that affect individuals. However, increasing transparency often comes at the cost of efficiency, as simpler, more interpretable models may be less powerful than complex deep learning systems. The challenge is finding a balance between performance and accountability.

Privacy concerns are another major ethical issue in algorithmic decision-making. Many modern algorithms rely on extensive data collection to refine their predictions and recommendations. Social media algorithms track user behavior, browsing history, and engagement metrics to personalize content. Financial algorithms analyze spending patterns to assess creditworthiness. Healthcare AI systems process sensitive medical data to recommend treatments. While these applications can improve user experience and efficiency, they also raise concerns about data security and consent.

Ethical AI development requires strict data protection measures, including encryption, anonymization, and secure storage practices. Users should have control over how their data is collected and used, with clear options to opt out of certain tracking mechanisms. Privacy-preserving technologies, such as differential privacy and federated learning, offer potential solutions by allowing AI systems to learn from data without directly accessing or storing personal information. However, implementing these measures often conflicts with business models that rely on data-driven revenue, creating a tension between ethical responsibility and corporate profitability.

Another ethical challenge is the potential for algorithms to manipulate human behavior. Social media algorithms are designed to maximize engagement, often by promoting content that triggers strong emotional reactions. Outrage, sensationalism, and divisive content tend to generate higher engagement, leading algorithms to prioritize such material over more balanced or nuanced perspectives. This dynamic has contributed to the spread of misinformation, political polarization, and addictive social media behaviors.

To make algorithms more ethical, platforms must shift their focus from engagement maximization to well-being optimization. Some researchers advocate for algorithms that promote digital literacy, encourage critical thinking, and prioritize content diversity. Platforms could introduce features that allow users to customize their algorithmic feeds, choosing whether they want to see content ranked by engagement, chronological order, or informational accuracy. However, these changes require a fundamental shift in how social media companies operate, as their current revenue models depend on maximizing user time spent on their platforms.

Accountability in algorithmic decision-making is another critical aspect of ethical AI. When an algorithm produces harmful outcomes—such as discriminatory hiring practices, biased policing, or the spread of false information—who is responsible? Unlike human decision-makers, algorithms do not have moral agency, making it difficult to assign blame when things go wrong. Companies that deploy AI systems often shift responsibility onto the algorithm itself, avoiding direct accountability.

To address this issue, ethical AI frameworks must include clear mechanisms for human oversight and redress. Users should have the ability to appeal algorithmic decisions, with human moderators available to review cases where AI systems fail. Governments and regulatory bodies are beginning to introduce legal frameworks that hold companies accountable for the consequences of their algorithms. Some experts propose independent AI ethics boards or algorithmic audit systems to assess and certify AI models before deployment.

Establishing clear lines of responsibility will be essential to ensuring that AI systems operate in ways that align with human values.

The question of whether truly ethical algorithms can exist remains open-ended. Ethical considerations in AI development often involve trade-offs between competing values, such as accuracy versus fairness, transparency versus efficiency, and privacy versus personalization. While no algorithm can be entirely free of bias, harm, or unintended consequences, efforts can be made to minimize negative impacts and align AI development with ethical principles.

Collaboration between technologists, ethicists, policymakers, and civil society will be crucial in shaping the future of ethical AI. Establishing global standards for algorithmic transparency, fairness, and accountability can help create guidelines that ensure AI systems serve the public good. Additionally, educating users about how algorithms work and how they influence decisions can empower individuals to navigate digital environments more critically.

As artificial intelligence continues to evolve, ethical considerations will become even more critical in determining how these technologies integrate into society. By prioritizing fairness, transparency, privacy, and accountability, developers can work toward creating AI systems that are not only powerful but also responsible. Ethical AI is not just a technological challenge—it is a societal one, requiring ongoing dialogue, oversight, and commitment to ensuring that algorithms enhance human well-being rather than exploit it.

Privacy Concerns in the Age of Algorithmic Social Media

The rise of algorithmic social media has transformed the way people interact online, offering highly personalized experiences tailored to individual preferences. These algorithms analyze vast amounts of data to predict what content users will engage with, optimizing feeds for maximum attention and interaction. While this personalization enhances user experience, it comes at the cost of privacy. Social media platforms collect, store, and analyze extensive personal data, raising concerns about surveillance, data security, consent, and the ethical implications of algorithm-driven engagement. The increasing reliance on artificial intelligence to shape digital interactions has made privacy a growing concern, as users have little control over how their data is used and shared.

One of the primary privacy concerns in algorithmic social media is the sheer scale of data collection. Every click, like, share, and comment is tracked to build detailed user profiles. Beyond direct interactions, platforms monitor time spent on posts, scroll patterns, and even pauses in browsing to refine their understanding of user behavior. Many social media networks collect location data, device information, and browsing history, even when users are not actively engaging with the platform. This data collection extends beyond what users knowingly provide, creating an ecosystem where personal information is constantly harvested, often without explicit consent.

Algorithmic profiling is another major issue, as social media platforms use collected data to categorize users based on interests, political beliefs, purchasing behavior, and social connections. These profiles influence what content is shown, what ads are targeted, and even what job opportunities or financial offers are presented. While some users appreciate the convenience of personalized recommendations, others see it as a violation of privacy, as their online behavior is used to shape their digital experiences in ways they may not fully understand. This profiling raises ethical concerns about autonomy, as individuals are nudged toward specific content, opinions, and commercial decisions without realizing the extent of algorithmic influence.

Social media tracking extends far beyond individual platforms, following users across the internet. Many websites incorporate tracking pixels, cookies, and embedded scripts that allow social media companies to collect data on users' activities outside their platforms. Facebook's Pixel, Google Analytics, and similar tracking tools monitor browsing habits, purchases, and search queries, integrating this information into user profiles. Even users who do not have accounts on certain platforms can be tracked through shadow profiles, where data from friends, contacts, and public records is used to build hidden profiles. This level of surveillance creates a scenario where digital privacy is nearly impossible, as personal information is continuously gathered and linked across multiple platforms and services.

Data security is another significant concern, as massive amounts of personal information are stored by social media companies. High-profile data breaches have exposed millions of user accounts, revealing sensitive details such as email addresses, passwords, private messages, and browsing histories. Hackers, cybercriminals, and even government agencies have exploited these breaches, accessing data that can be used for identity theft, blackmail, or political manipulation. When user data is leaked, it becomes nearly impossible to erase from the internet, leaving individuals vulnerable to long-term privacy risks. Despite promises from tech companies to strengthen security measures, data breaches continue to occur, highlighting the risks of entrusting vast amounts of personal information to centralized corporate entities.

Facial recognition and biometric data collection present additional privacy risks. Many social media platforms have experimented with AI-driven facial recognition, enabling automatic tagging in photos, security features, and targeted advertising. While these tools offer convenience, they also enable mass surveillance, allowing companies and governments to track individuals based on facial data. In some cases, social media companies have been accused of collecting biometric data without user consent, leading to legal challenges and regulatory scrutiny. The increasing integration of biometric tracking raises ethical concerns about consent, as users often have little control over how their facial data is stored and used.

Privacy policies on social media platforms are often opaque and difficult to navigate, making it challenging for users to understand what data is being collected and how it is being used. Many platforms use vague language in their policies, allowing for broad interpretations that enable extensive data collection and sharing with third parties. Even when privacy controls are available, they are often hidden behind multiple settings, requiring users to take extensive steps to limit data tracking. The complexity of these policies discourages users from taking control of their data, leading to passive acceptance of invasive data practices.

Governments and regulatory bodies have begun implementing laws to address privacy concerns in algorithmic social media. The European Union's General Data Protection Regulation (GDPR) requires companies to disclose data collection practices, provide users with access to their stored information, and offer options for data deletion. Similarly, the California Consumer Privacy Act (CCPA) grants users the right to opt out of data sales and demand greater transparency from companies. While these regulations represent progress, enforcement remains inconsistent, and tech companies often find ways to comply with the letter of the law while continuing to collect vast amounts of user data.

Despite growing awareness of privacy risks, many users continue to engage with social media without fully understanding the extent of data tracking. The convenience of algorithmically curated feeds, targeted ads, and seamless digital interactions often outweighs concerns about surveillance. Additionally, the dominance of social media in communication, business, and entertainment makes it difficult for individuals to disconnect completely. Some users take steps to protect their privacy, using ad blockers, virtual private networks (VPNs), and privacy-focused browsers, but these solutions require technical knowledge and do not fully eliminate tracking. The reality is that opting out of algorithmic surveillance is not a practical option for most people in a world where social media is deeply integrated into daily life.

Social media companies have introduced limited privacy-focused features, but these often serve as superficial solutions rather than meaningful reforms. Some platforms allow users to opt out of targeted ads, restrict data sharing with third parties, or enable encrypted messaging. However, these features do not address the fundamental issue of data collection, as the core business model of social media relies on harvesting user information for advertising revenue. While privacy-conscious users can take advantage of these tools, true data protection would require a shift away from engagement-driven advertising models, something most tech companies are unwilling to consider.

The future of privacy in algorithmic social media will depend on a combination of regulatory action, corporate responsibility, and user awareness. Governments may introduce stricter laws requiring companies to limit data collection and provide greater transparency. Tech companies could adopt privacy-first business models, prioritizing user control over data monetization. Users themselves can demand better protections, advocating for stronger privacy rights and holding platforms accountable for their practices. As artificial intelligence and machine learning continue to evolve, privacy concerns will become even more pressing, shaping the next era of digital communication.

Algorithmic social media has redefined privacy in ways that most users never anticipated. The trade-off between convenience and personal data exposure has become a central issue in the digital age, forcing individuals, companies, and governments to reconsider what privacy means in an era of constant surveillance. While complete privacy in social media may be unrealistic, greater transparency, user control, and regulatory oversight could help create a more ethical and privacy-conscious digital environment. The challenge is not just protecting personal data but ensuring that users retain agency over their online experiences in a world increasingly shaped by algorithmic decision-making.

How AI-Powered Algorithms Shape Trends

AI-powered algorithms have become the driving force behind digital trends, determining what content goes viral, which topics dominate discussions, and how consumer behaviors shift in response to emerging cultural phenomena. These algorithms operate across social media platforms, search engines, streaming services, and e-commerce sites, analyzing user behavior to predict and amplify content that is likely to generate high engagement. What appears to be organic popularity is often the result of highly sophisticated AI systems that detect patterns, adjust recommendations, and continuously refine their models based on user interactions. The influence of AI in shaping trends extends beyond entertainment and commerce into politics, social movements, and public discourse, making it one of the most powerful forces in the modern digital landscape.

At the core of AI-driven trend formation is the ability of algorithms to track and analyze massive amounts of user data. Every like, comment, share, and view contributes to the machine learning models that determine what content is promoted. These models identify patterns in engagement, predicting which topics are likely to gain momentum. Once a piece of content starts to show signs of virality—whether through rapid interactions, increased watch time, or high comment activity—the algorithm boosts its visibility, exposing it to more users and accelerating its spread. This feedback loop ensures that the most engaging content reaches the widest audience, often making it seem as though trends emerge spontaneously when, in reality, they are being reinforced by AI systems optimizing for maximum reach.

One of the most visible ways AI shapes trends is through social media feeds. Platforms like TikTok, Instagram, Twitter, and YouTube use recommendation algorithms that prioritize content based on predicted user interest rather than chronological order. TikTok's For You Page is particularly influential in this regard, using deep learning models to push videos that align with individual viewing behaviors. Unlike traditional social networks that rely heavily on follower counts, TikTok's AI enables even small creators to go viral if their content resonates with audience engagement patterns. This democratization of trend formation allows for rapid shifts in online culture, where new challenges, memes, dances, and catchphrases can rise to prominence within days.

Music trends are heavily shaped by AI-powered algorithms that drive discovery and streaming habits. TikTok, Spotify, and YouTube analyze listening patterns and engagement metrics to determine which songs should be recommended to larger audiences. TikTok's algorithm, in particular, has the ability to turn previously obscure songs into global hits by amplifying videos that use them as background music. Record labels and artists now design music with social media virality in mind, creating tracks that fit TikTok's short-form video format. Spotify's AI-driven playlists, such as Discover Weekly and Release Radar, further influence listening trends by predicting what users are most likely to enjoy based on past behavior. The result is a music industry where AI plays a significant role in determining which songs succeed and which fade into obscurity.

Fashion and beauty trends are also increasingly dictated by AI algorithms that analyze image recognition data, shopping behaviors, and influencer interactions. Platforms like Instagram and Pinterest use AI to detect visual patterns and promote specific aesthetics to users who have engaged with similar content. AI-driven fashion recommendation engines track consumer preferences, predicting upcoming trends based on search history and purchase patterns. Fast fashion brands leverage these insights to rapidly produce clothing lines that align with trending styles, shortening the time between digital trend emergence and retail availability. AI-generated virtual influencers further blur the line between human-driven and algorithmically curated fashion trends, as digital avatars designed by AI gain popularity on social media.

E-commerce platforms use AI to shape consumer trends by personalizing recommendations and predicting future demand. Amazon, for example, uses machine learning to analyze browsing history, past purchases, and product reviews to suggest items that users are likely to buy. This predictive shopping model ensures that trending products receive greater visibility, reinforcing consumer interest and driving demand. Similarly, AI-powered chatbots and virtual assistants guide purchasing decisions by suggesting products tailored to individual preferences. The integration of AI in e-commerce has created a cycle where user behavior informs algorithmic recommendations, which in turn influence purchasing decisions, further solidifying trends.

Beyond consumer culture, AI-powered algorithms play a role in shaping political and social trends. Social media platforms prioritize content that generates high engagement, which often includes politically charged discussions, controversial topics, and social justice movements. The algorithms do not distinguish between positive or negative engagement, meaning that outrage and support alike contribute to a trend's visibility. Movements such as #MeToo, Black Lives Matter, and climate activism have gained global traction through AI-driven amplification. At the same time, misinformation and propaganda campaigns can exploit these same algorithms to spread false narratives, manipulate public opinion, and influence elections. The ability of AI to elevate certain political narratives over others has sparked debates about algorithmic responsibility and the role of technology in democratic processes.

AI's influence on news trends is evident in how search engines and news aggregators rank stories. Google's search algorithm determines which news articles appear first based on factors such as relevance, engagement, and site authority. Social media platforms use AI to recommend trending news topics, often favoring sensational headlines that drive higher click-through rates. The rise of AI-generated news summaries and automated journalism further complicates information consumption, as algorithms are now capable of synthesizing and distributing news without direct human editorial oversight. While this enhances the speed and efficiency of news delivery, it also raises concerns about bias, accuracy, and the potential for AI-driven misinformation.

The entertainment industry is experiencing a shift where AI-driven algorithms dictate content trends across streaming services, gaming platforms, and digital media. Netflix, Hulu, and Disney+ use machine learning to recommend shows and movies based on viewing history, influencing what audiences watch and shaping demand for certain genres and storytelling formats. Video game developers use AI to track player behavior, optimizing in-game recommendations and content updates to align with engagement patterns. AI-generated content, such as deepfake influencers and virtual reality experiences, further expands the possibilities of entertainment trends driven by algorithmic decision-making.

As AI continues to evolve, its role in shaping trends will become even more sophisticated. Predictive modeling will allow platforms to anticipate trends before they fully emerge, influencing everything from fashion cycles to political movements in real time. AI-generated content, such as art, music, and literature, will further challenge traditional notions of creativity, as machine learning models become capable of producing works that rival human-generated material. The increasing integration of AI into everyday life means that digital trends will be less about organic cultural movements and more about algorithmically optimized patterns designed to maximize engagement and influence behavior.

AI-powered algorithms have redefined how trends emerge, spread, and evolve. Whether in entertainment, consumer behavior, politics, or social movements, AI plays an active role in curating and amplifying digital culture. While these systems create opportunities for innovation and discovery, they also raise concerns about manipulation, bias, and the unintended consequences of algorithmic influence. As technology advances, the balance between AI-driven optimization and human agency will shape the future of digital trends, determining whether they remain reflections of organic interest or become increasingly engineered by the invisible hands of artificial intelligence.

The Battle Against Algorithmic Manipulation

The increasing reliance on algorithmic systems to curate content, make decisions, and influence public opinion has led to a growing concern over algorithmic manipulation. As social media platforms, search engines, and digital marketplaces use artificial intelligence to optimize engagement and maximize revenue, various actors—including individuals, corporations, and state-sponsored groups—seek to exploit these systems for personal, political, or financial gain. Algorithmic manipulation distorts online ecosystems, undermining trust in digital platforms and creating challenges for regulators, platform owners, and everyday users. The battle against this form of manipulation is complex, requiring a combination of technological solutions, policy interventions, and digital literacy efforts to protect the integrity of online spaces.

One of the most prevalent forms of algorithmic manipulation is the use of bots and automated engagement tools to amplify content artificially. Social media bots are designed to mimic human behavior, liking, sharing, and commenting on posts to increase their visibility within algorithm-driven recommendation systems. These bots can be deployed to boost a brand's popularity, manipulate public sentiment, or spread misinformation. Political campaigns, advocacy groups, and businesses have used bot networks to create the illusion of widespread support for certain ideas, products, or candidates. By flooding platforms with artificial engagement, these actors trick algorithms into promoting specific narratives, making them appear more organic and widely accepted than they actually are.

Click farms and coordinated engagement rings also contribute to algorithmic manipulation. Click farms employ low-wage workers who manually interact with content to simulate genuine engagement, inflating metrics such as views, likes, and followers. Engagement rings operate on a more decentralized level, where groups of users agree to like and share each other's content to boost algorithmic ranking. These tactics are commonly used by influencers trying to gain visibility, businesses looking to increase brand awareness, and individuals seeking social validation. While platform policies prohibit such practices, enforcement remains difficult, as many of these activities appear indistinguishable from normal user behavior.

Misinformation campaigns are another major area of concern when it comes to algorithmic manipulation. AI-driven content recommendation systems prioritize engagement, which often leads to the spread of sensationalist, misleading, or emotionally charged content. Bad actors exploit this dynamic by creating false narratives designed to provoke strong reactions, knowing that engagement-driven algorithms will amplify them. State-sponsored disinformation campaigns, conspiracy theorists, and financially motivated actors use algorithmic weaknesses to spread misleading content, influencing public opinion on topics ranging from elections and public health to social movements and global events. The challenge for platforms is filtering out manipulated content without infringing on free speech or unintentionally suppressing legitimate discourse.

Deepfake technology has introduced a new dimension to algorithmic manipulation. AI-generated videos and images can depict people saying or doing things they never actually did, making it increasingly difficult to distinguish between real and manipulated content. When combined with algorithmic amplification, deepfakes can be weaponized for political propaganda, character assassination, or financial fraud. The potential for deepfake-driven manipulation has led to growing concerns over digital trust, as users struggle to verify the authenticity of online content. Efforts to develop AI tools capable of detecting deepfakes remain ongoing, but the technology continues to evolve, making detection an ongoing arms race between developers and malicious actors.

Social media platforms have introduced various measures to combat algorithmic manipulation, but challenges persist. AI-driven moderation systems scan for inauthentic engagement patterns, identifying and removing bot accounts, click farms, and coordinated manipulation efforts. However, these detection systems are not perfect, often resulting in false positives where legitimate users are penalized or false negatives where manipulative tactics go undetected. Additionally, algorithmic updates designed to counter manipulation can have unintended consequences, sometimes altering content distribution in ways that disproportionately affect certain groups or perspectives.

Fact-checking initiatives have been deployed to address misinformation, with platforms partnering with independent organizations to verify content and flag false information. While this approach helps limit the spread of disinformation, it faces resistance from users who distrust fact-checking entities or perceive moderation efforts as biased. Some platforms use warning labels to indicate potentially misleading content, reducing its visibility without outright removing it. However, the effectiveness of such measures is debated, as flagged content often continues to spread within echo chambers where algorithmic recommendations reinforce preexisting beliefs.

Transparency efforts aim to give users more insight into how algorithms function and how content is ranked. Some platforms have introduced tools that allow users to see why certain posts are recommended, providing explanations based on engagement history and personalization factors. Regulators and advocacy groups have called for even greater transparency, demanding that platforms disclose the criteria used for content ranking and algorithmic decision-making. However, companies often resist full transparency, citing concerns about proprietary technology and the risk of exploitation by bad actors seeking to game the system further.

Regulatory interventions have begun shaping the battle against algorithmic manipulation. Governments have introduced laws requiring platforms to take greater responsibility for algorithmic content distribution, ensuring that automated systems do not enable fraud, disinformation, or election interference. Some jurisdictions have proposed regulations that mandate algorithmic audits, allowing independent experts to evaluate whether platform algorithms are being manipulated or producing harmful outcomes. While these efforts represent progress, regulation remains challenging due to the global nature of digital platforms and the rapid pace of technological advancement.

User awareness and digital literacy are essential components in the fight against algorithmic manipulation. Many users are unaware of how algorithms shape their online experiences, making them vulnerable to manipulation tactics. Efforts to educate users on how recommendation systems work, how to identify suspicious content, and how to critically evaluate online information can help reduce the effectiveness of manipulation strategies. Schools, media organizations, and advocacy groups have developed digital literacy programs aimed at teaching users to recognize bots, fact-check information, and navigate online spaces more responsibly.

Despite ongoing efforts to combat algorithmic manipulation, the challenge remains dynamic, as bad actors continuously adapt their tactics to evade detection. As artificial intelligence becomes more sophisticated, the potential for manipulation will only grow, requiring platforms, regulators, and users to remain vigilant. Striking a balance between maintaining free expression, ensuring algorithmic fairness, and preventing the abuse of automated systems will be critical in shaping the future of digital interactions. The battle against algorithmic manipulation is not just a technological issue but a societal one, requiring cooperation across industries, governments, and individuals to ensure that digital platforms serve as trustworthy spaces for information and communication.

How Algorithms Affect Journalism and News Distribution

Algorithms have become central to how news is distributed, consumed, and monetized in the digital age. As traditional news outlets have shifted online, the role of search engines, social media platforms, and content aggregators in shaping journalism has expanded dramatically. Algorithms determine which articles appear in search results, what news stories are featured on social media feeds, and how widely different types of reporting are distributed. While these automated systems provide efficiency and personalization, they also introduce challenges related to bias, misinformation, financial sustainability, and the overall role of journalism in society. The influence of algorithms on news distribution has fundamentally reshaped the information ecosystem, creating both opportunities and ethical dilemmas for media organizations, journalists, and readers.

Search engine algorithms play a major role in determining which news sources gain visibility. Google, the dominant search engine, uses sophisticated ranking algorithms to decide which articles appear at the top of search results. These algorithms evaluate factors such as relevance, website authority, user engagement, and the freshness of the content. News outlets that optimize their articles for search engine optimization (SEO) have a greater chance of reaching wider audiences. However, this has led to changes in journalistic practices, as many publications tailor their headlines, keywords, and article structures to align with search engine preferences rather than journalistic integrity. The pressure to rank higher in search results has pushed some media organizations to prioritize speed and virality over depth and accuracy.

Social media algorithms have further transformed news distribution by curating personalized feeds based on user behavior. Platforms like Facebook, Twitter, and Instagram use machine learning to determine what content to prioritize for each individual user. Engagement-driven algorithms amplify news stories that generate high interaction rates, favoring emotionally charged headlines, sensationalism, and controversy. This mechanism can lead to the rapid spread of viral news, but it also creates an environment where clickbait and misinformation thrive. Since algorithms optimize for engagement rather than journalistic quality, serious investigative reporting may struggle to gain visibility compared to emotionally compelling but less fact-driven content.

The shift toward algorithm-driven news distribution has also changed how journalists and media companies operate. Many newsrooms now analyze audience data to tailor their content to what algorithms favor. Headlines are crafted to maximize clicks, article structures are adjusted to increase readability scores, and publication schedules are optimized for peak algorithmic reach. While this data-driven approach has helped some media organizations grow their online presence, it has also led to concerns about editorial independence. Journalistic decisions that were once based on editorial judgment and public interest are now increasingly influenced by algorithmic trends, shaping the types of stories that get covered and how they are presented.

The financial sustainability of journalism has also been affected by algorithmic news distribution. Traditional revenue models based on newspaper subscriptions and print advertising have declined, forcing media companies to rely more on digital advertising and social media traffic. However, advertising revenue is largely controlled by tech giants such as Google and Facebook, which use their algorithms to direct ad placement and revenue distribution. Many news organizations depend on traffic from these platforms to generate ad revenue, making them vulnerable to changes in algorithms that reduce their visibility. Sudden shifts in platform policies, such as Facebook's decision to deprioritize news content in its feed, have had severe financial consequences for digital media outlets.

Misinformation and the spread of fake news have been exacerbated by algorithmic news distribution. Since engagement-based ranking systems prioritize content that elicits strong reactions, false or misleading information often spreads faster than verified journalism. Studies have shown that fake news stories, particularly those related to politics, health, and conspiracy theories, receive more shares and interactions than factual reporting. Social media platforms have implemented fact-checking initiatives and content moderation policies to combat misinformation, but these efforts have been met with mixed success. Algorithms struggle to differentiate between nuanced, fact-based reporting and misleading content designed to manipulate public opinion.

Filter bubbles and echo chambers have emerged as another unintended consequence of algorithmic news distribution. Since algorithms personalize content based on past behavior, users are often exposed to news that reinforces their existing beliefs while filtering out opposing perspectives. This creates ideological echo chambers where people are only presented with information that aligns with their biases, reducing exposure to diverse viewpoints and critical analysis. The fragmentation of news consumption has contributed to increased polarization, as individuals engage primarily with content that supports their worldview. Efforts to introduce algorithmic diversity by incorporating alternative perspectives into news feeds have faced resistance, as users tend to engage more with content that confirms their opinions.

Efforts to improve algorithmic news distribution have included transparency initiatives and regulatory proposals. Some platforms have introduced tools that allow users to see why certain news stories appear in their feeds, offering greater insight into how algorithms make decisions. Google's AI-driven journalism projects aim to support high-quality reporting by funding investigative journalism and developing AI tools that assist newsrooms. However, critics argue that these measures do not go far enough in addressing the structural issues caused by algorithmic influence over news distribution. Policymakers in various countries have proposed regulations requiring platforms to provide greater algorithmic transparency, ensure fair revenue distribution for news publishers, and take stronger action against misinformation.

Alternative models for news distribution that reduce algorithmic dependence have also emerged. Subscription-based journalism has gained popularity, with outlets like The New York Times, The Washington Post, and The Guardian shifting toward reader-supported funding models. Crowdfunding platforms allow independent journalists to bypass algorithm-driven monetization entirely, relying on direct audience contributions. Some media organizations have explored blockchain-based news distribution systems that decentralize content distribution, reducing reliance on tech giants. While these models offer potential solutions, they require cultural shifts in how audiences consume and pay for news.

The long-term impact of algorithmic news distribution remains uncertain. As AI systems become more advanced, they may refine content curation to prioritize accuracy, credibility, and balanced reporting. However, the profit-driven nature of tech platforms means that engagement and advertising revenue will likely continue to shape algorithmic priorities. The challenge for journalists, media organizations, and regulators is finding ways to align digital news distribution with the core principles of journalism: accuracy, accountability, and public interest. The relationship between algorithms and journalism will continue to evolve, influencing not only how news is consumed but also the role of the press in shaping public discourse and democracy.

The Relationship Between Algorithms and User Behavior

Algorithms have fundamentally transformed the way people interact with digital content, shaping not only what they see but also how they behave online. Social media platforms, search engines, streaming services, and e-commerce websites use sophisticated machine learning models to analyze user behavior, predict preferences, and personalize experiences. This constant feedback loop between algorithms and users has created an ecosystem where digital interactions are increasingly influenced by automated systems that learn and adapt in real-time. While these algorithms are designed to enhance user experience and engagement, they also raise important questions about autonomy, decision-making, and the unintended consequences of algorithmic influence.

One of the primary ways algorithms influence user behavior is through content curation. Platforms such as Facebook, Instagram, Twitter, and TikTok use recommendation algorithms to decide which posts, videos, and news articles appear in a user's feed. These systems analyze past interactions, engagement history, and browsing patterns to determine what content is most likely to capture attention. As a result, users are not just passively consuming content; they are being guided toward specific types of media that align with their preferences and past behaviors. Over time, this creates a reinforcing cycle where individuals are repeatedly exposed to similar content, strengthening existing interests and reducing exposure to diverse perspectives.

Personalization is often framed as a benefit, as it allows users to see content that is relevant to them. However, the downside of hyper-personalization is that it can create echo chambers and filter bubbles, where users are only shown information that confirms their existing beliefs. This effect is particularly evident in political discourse, where algorithm-driven feeds prioritize content that generates strong emotional reactions. By promoting highly engaging content, algorithms can inadvertently contribute to ideological polarization, as users become less likely to encounter viewpoints that challenge their perspectives. This narrowing of informational exposure has significant implications for public discourse, critical thinking, and democratic decision-making.

The way users engage with content also directly influences algorithmic recommendations. Every like, comment, share, and click serves as a data point that helps refine future content suggestions. Platforms prioritize posts that generate high engagement, creating an environment where users are incentivized to produce content that aligns with algorithmic preferences. This has led to the rise of content strategies designed to maximize algorithmic visibility, with creators optimizing their posts for trends, hashtags, and engagement triggers. The pursuit of algorithmic success has shaped digital culture, encouraging formats such as clickbait headlines, reaction videos, and short-form viral challenges. While this gamification of content creation drives platform growth, it also alters user behavior, as individuals adapt their online interactions to fit within the parameters set by algorithms.

Another significant impact of algorithmic influence is on attention spans and digital consumption habits. Platforms like TikTok and YouTube rely on AI-driven recommendation engines to keep users engaged for as long as possible. The infinite scrolling feature, autoplay functions, and real-time content adjustments create an experience where users can effortlessly consume content without making active choices. This passive consumption model encourages binge-watching, doomscrolling, and prolonged screen time, reinforcing habits that prioritize instant gratification over intentional content discovery. Studies have suggested that these algorithm-driven behaviors may contribute to decreased attention spans, as users become accustomed to rapidly switching between pieces of content without sustained focus.

Algorithms also shape user behavior in more subtle ways through behavioral nudging. Social media platforms use machine learning to predict which notifications, alerts, or suggested interactions will increase user engagement. By strategically timing push notifications, reminding users of unread messages, or suggesting content at peak hours, algorithms guide individuals toward specific actions that benefit platform engagement metrics. These subtle nudges create compulsive usage patterns, where users feel a constant pull to check their devices, respond to notifications, and stay connected to algorithmically curated feeds. This design approach has raised concerns about digital addiction, as the mechanics of algorithmic engagement encourage continuous, sometimes unhealthy, interaction with digital platforms.

The commercial implications of algorithmic influence extend beyond social media into areas such as online shopping, entertainment, and lifestyle choices. E-commerce platforms like Amazon use AI-driven recommendation engines to predict what products users are likely to buy based on browsing history, past purchases, and demographic data. By suggesting products that align with user preferences, these algorithms not only enhance convenience but also subtly shape consumer behavior, steering users toward specific purchasing decisions. Similarly, streaming services such as Netflix and Spotify curate content based on past interactions, influencing what users watch and listen to without them actively searching for new material. The more users interact with algorithm-driven recommendations, the more their behavior conforms to the patterns predicted by AI, reinforcing the system's influence over time.

Despite the significant impact of algorithms on user behavior, most people are unaware of the extent to which their online experiences are shaped by machine learning. The opacity of algorithmic decision-making means that users often do not realize why they are seeing certain content or why their digital habits change over time. Some platforms have introduced transparency measures, such as showing users why a post appears in their feed or providing options to adjust recommendation settings. However, these features are often buried within platform settings, making it difficult for users to fully understand or control how algorithms shape their experiences.

The ethical implications of algorithm-driven behavior modification have sparked debates about the responsibility of tech companies in designing AI systems that prioritize user well-being. Some experts argue that platforms should develop algorithms that promote healthier digital habits, such as encouraging breaks from prolonged screen time or prioritizing content that fosters meaningful interactions over engagement maximization. Others advocate for greater user control, where individuals can customize their algorithmic preferences, choosing what factors influence their content recommendations. While some platforms have introduced features that allow users to switch to chronological feeds or limit notifications, the broader industry remains largely focused on optimizing engagement rather than ethical algorithmic design.

As artificial intelligence continues to advance, the relationship between algorithms and user behavior will become even more complex. The next generation of AI-driven systems may incorporate more sophisticated behavioral predictions, emotional analysis, and real-time adaptation, further refining their ability to shape user actions. This raises important questions about agency, autonomy, and the long-term impact of algorithmic influence on human decision-making. The challenge for technology companies, regulators, and society at large is to ensure that algorithmic systems are designed not just for efficiency and profitability but also for the well-being and empowerment of users. Recognizing how algorithms shape behavior is the first step toward creating a more transparent and ethical digital environment where users retain greater control over their online experiences.

The Role of Governments in Regulating Algorithms

Governments around the world are facing growing pressure to regulate algorithms as these automated systems increasingly influence daily life. From social media feeds and search engine rankings to financial decisions and law enforcement practices, algorithms shape the way information is distributed, how businesses operate, and even how justice is administered. While these technologies provide efficiency and scalability, they also introduce risks related to bias, misinformation, privacy violations, and lack of accountability. The challenge for governments is to create regulations that ensure fairness, transparency, and ethical use of algorithms without stifling innovation or infringing on free speech.

One of the main concerns driving government intervention is algorithmic bias. Many machine learning models are trained on historical data that reflects societal inequalities. This means that algorithms used in hiring, lending, and law enforcement may unintentionally discriminate against marginalized groups. Cases of racial and gender bias in AI-driven recruitment tools, credit scoring systems, and predictive policing have raised alarms about the need for regulatory oversight. Governments have responded by introducing laws that require companies to conduct bias audits and ensure that their algorithms comply with anti-discrimination standards. Some jurisdictions have gone further by mandating fairness assessments before an algorithm is deployed, ensuring that automated decision-making does not reinforce existing inequalities.

Privacy protection is another major area of concern. Social media platforms, e-commerce websites, and digital advertisers rely on algorithms to collect, analyze, and monetize vast amounts of personal data. Governments have introduced data protection laws to limit how much personal information companies can collect and store. The European Union's General Data Protection Regulation (GDPR) and the California Consumer Privacy Act (CCPA) give users more control over their data, allowing them to request access, deletion, or correction of personal information. These regulations also require companies to be transparent about how their algorithms use personal data, reducing the risk of unauthorized surveillance and data exploitation.

The spread of misinformation and the role of algorithms in amplifying false or misleading content have prompted governments to consider stricter regulations for social media platforms. Algorithm-driven recommendation systems prioritize engagement, often boosting sensational, emotionally charged, or polarizing content. This dynamic has contributed to the rapid spread of fake news, conspiracy theories, and political propaganda. Some governments have introduced laws that hold platforms accountable for the content they promote, requiring them to take proactive steps to reduce misinformation. However, regulating online speech raises complex ethical questions about free expression, as efforts to curb harmful content can sometimes lead to accusations of censorship. Policymakers must find a balance between preventing algorithmic amplification of false information and preserving open discourse.

Transparency in algorithmic decision-making is another area where governments have stepped in. Many algorithms function as black boxes, meaning that their decision-making processes are not easily understood or explained. This lack of transparency creates challenges when users are affected by algorithmic outcomes, such as being denied a loan or having their social media content suppressed without clear justification. Some governments have proposed regulations that require companies to disclose how their algorithms work, including the factors that influence automated decisions. Algorithmic transparency laws aim to provide greater accountability, ensuring that users have recourse when they are negatively impacted by AI-driven decisions.

Governments have also turned their attention to the role of algorithms in shaping market competition. Large technology companies that control powerful algorithms often dominate entire industries, making it difficult for smaller competitors to gain visibility. Search engine algorithms prioritize certain results, e-commerce platforms favor their own products, and social media algorithms amplify content from high-profile accounts. Regulators have launched antitrust investigations to determine whether these practices constitute unfair competition. Some policymakers have proposed laws that would require tech companies to ensure fair algorithmic treatment of competitors, preventing dominant platforms from using their algorithms to reinforce their market power.

Another critical area of regulation is the use of AI-driven algorithms in law enforcement and criminal justice. Predictive policing algorithms analyze historical crime data to determine where law enforcement resources should be deployed. While these systems aim to improve efficiency, studies have shown that they often reinforce racial and socioeconomic biases. Facial recognition technology, which is increasingly used by law enforcement agencies, has been criticized for its inaccuracies and potential for misuse. Some governments have banned the use of facial recognition in public spaces, while others have introduced strict guidelines on how AI-driven surveillance tools can be used. These regulatory efforts seek to prevent algorithmic discrimination while ensuring that law enforcement agencies remain accountable for their use of AI technologies.

Financial regulations have also expanded to include oversight of algorithmic decision-making in banking, lending, and insurance. Automated credit scoring models determine whether individuals qualify for loans, while AI-driven fraud detection systems monitor financial transactions for suspicious activity. Governments have introduced regulations requiring financial institutions to explain how algorithmic decisions are made and to ensure that these systems do not unfairly disadvantage certain groups. Some regulatory bodies have mandated that financial algorithms undergo regular audits to identify and mitigate discriminatory practices. Ensuring fairness and transparency in financial AI systems is essential to preventing economic disparities driven by algorithmic biases.

The challenge of regulating algorithms is compounded by the rapid pace of technological advancement. AI models evolve continuously, making it difficult for policymakers to create regulations that remain relevant over time. Many governments are adopting flexible regulatory approaches that allow for ongoing updates and adjustments as technology develops. Some have proposed the creation of independent AI oversight bodies that specialize in algorithmic accountability, conducting audits, issuing guidelines, and recommending policy changes. These regulatory frameworks aim to strike a balance between fostering innovation and protecting the public from harmful algorithmic practices.

Global coordination in algorithmic regulation is another challenge. While some countries have introduced strict AI laws, others have taken a more hands-off approach, creating inconsistencies in how algorithms are governed across different regions. International organizations have begun working toward common AI ethics guidelines to establish a baseline for responsible algorithmic use. However, enforcing these guidelines remains difficult, as tech companies operate across multiple jurisdictions with varying legal requirements. The development of global standards for algorithmic transparency, fairness, and accountability will be crucial in addressing cross-border challenges related to AI regulation.

Governments must also consider the impact of algorithmic regulations on innovation. While oversight is necessary to prevent harmful practices, overly restrictive regulations could stifle technological progress and limit the development of AI-driven solutions that benefit society. Striking the right balance between regulation and innovation requires collaboration between policymakers, tech companies, researchers, and civil society. Many governments have launched AI ethics initiatives that bring together stakeholders to develop policies that promote responsible AI development while allowing room for technological advancement.

As artificial intelligence continues to evolve, the role of governments in regulating algorithms will become increasingly important. Policymakers must ensure that algorithmic systems are designed and deployed in ways that align with ethical principles, protect individual rights, and promote fairness. While challenges remain in balancing transparency, accountability, and innovation, regulatory frameworks that prioritize responsible AI development will help shape a future where algorithms serve the public good rather than exacerbating social inequalities. The effectiveness of government intervention will depend on the willingness of regulators, industry leaders, and the public to work together in developing policies that ensure algorithms are used in ways that benefit society while minimizing their risks.

Algorithm Transparency: What We Know and What We Don't

Algorithms play a crucial role in shaping the digital world, determining what users see on social media, which search results appear first, and even influencing decisions related to hiring, healthcare, and finance. Despite their widespread impact, many of these algorithms function as black boxes, meaning that their inner workings are not fully understood by the public or even the companies that deploy them. Algorithm transparency—the concept of making the decision-making processes of algorithms understandable and accountable—has become an increasingly important issue as concerns about bias, manipulation, misinformation, and ethical AI development continue to grow. While some information about how algorithms work is available, there are still significant gaps in knowledge that make it difficult to assess their fairness, effectiveness, and potential harm.

One of the main things we know about algorithms is that they are designed to optimize specific outcomes. Whether an algorithm is ranking search results, recommending content, or approving loan applications, it follows a set of rules based on predefined objectives. Machine learning models, which power many modern algorithms, analyze patterns in data to improve their predictions over time. However, the exact way these systems arrive at their conclusions is often unclear, particularly with deep learning models that process vast amounts of data through complex neural networks. The more sophisticated the algorithm, the harder it becomes to explain why it makes certain decisions, which raises concerns about accountability and fairness.

Companies that develop and use algorithms sometimes provide high-level explanations of how their systems work. Social media platforms, for example, have released general descriptions of how content ranking systems prioritize posts. YouTube has stated that its recommendation algorithm considers factors such as watch time, user preferences, and engagement history when suggesting videos. Instagram has explained that its feed ranking is influenced by a combination of past interactions, post popularity, and relationship strength between users. While these insights offer a basic understanding, they do not provide enough detail to fully understand the mechanics of these systems or their unintended consequences. The lack of transparency makes it difficult for researchers, regulators, and users to determine whether algorithms are being used responsibly.

Some governments and advocacy groups have pushed for greater transparency by requiring companies to disclose how their algorithms operate. The European Union's Digital Services Act includes provisions that require platforms to provide more insight into their recommendation systems. The General Data Protection Regulation (GDPR) grants users the right to receive explanations for automated decisions that affect them, such as being denied a loan or having a job application rejected. In the United States, discussions about AI regulation have focused on the need for algorithmic audits and impact assessments to ensure fairness and prevent discrimination. While these efforts have led to incremental improvements in transparency, many companies remain reluctant to reveal too much about their algorithms, citing concerns about trade secrets, competitive advantage, and the potential for exploitation by malicious actors.

Despite some progress, there is still much that remains unknown about how algorithms function in practice. Many AI systems rely on massive datasets that contain hidden biases, yet it is often unclear how these biases influence decision-making. Studies have shown that facial recognition algorithms have higher error rates for people with darker skin tones, job application algorithms sometimes favor male candidates over female candidates, and predictive policing tools disproportionately target minority communities. Without full transparency into how these models are trained and tested, it is difficult to assess the extent of algorithmic bias and determine what steps are being taken to address it.

Another major unknown is how frequently algorithms change and adapt over time. Social media platforms and search engines regularly update their ranking systems to improve user experience, combat spam, or adjust to new business priorities. However, these updates are rarely disclosed in detail, leaving content creators, businesses, and users struggling to understand why their visibility or engagement fluctuates. When platforms make sudden algorithmic changes, entire industries can be affected. Digital media companies that rely on traffic from search engines and social media may experience drastic drops in visitors overnight if an update deprioritizes their content. The lack of transparency around these changes creates uncertainty for those who depend on algorithm-driven visibility.

One area where transparency is particularly lacking is in the use of AI-driven moderation and content filtering. Many platforms use automated systems to detect and remove harmful content, such as hate speech, misinformation, and copyright violations. However, the criteria used by these systems are often unclear, and mistakes are common. Content moderation algorithms have been criticized for inconsistencies, such as removing legitimate political discussions while allowing harmful misinformation to spread. Users who have their content removed or accounts suspended often receive vague explanations, making it difficult to appeal decisions or understand what went wrong. Greater transparency in content moderation algorithms could help users navigate platform policies more effectively and hold companies accountable for errors.

The issue of algorithm transparency is further complicated by the rise of AI-generated content. As artificial intelligence becomes more capable of producing realistic images, videos, and text, distinguishing between human-created and machine-generated content has become increasingly difficult. Deepfake videos, AI-generated news articles, and synthetic voices pose challenges for information integrity, yet the algorithms that detect and regulate this content are not always disclosed. Platforms have introduced AI-generated content labels, but without clear guidelines on how these labels are applied, questions remain about their effectiveness and reliability. Transparency in AI detection algorithms is essential to maintaining trust in digital information.

While full transparency may not always be possible, there are steps that companies and policymakers can take to improve algorithmic accountability. One approach is requiring independent audits of AI systems to evaluate their fairness and potential biases. Researchers and advocacy groups have called for algorithmic explainability tools that provide users with clear, accessible explanations of why certain recommendations or decisions are made. Some have suggested implementing algorithmic choice features that allow users to adjust their own content preferences rather than relying entirely on platform-driven rankings. These measures could help bridge the gap between algorithmic complexity and user understanding.

The balance between transparency and security is another challenge. While disclosing algorithmic processes can help users and regulators understand their impact, too much openness could allow bad actors to manipulate systems for fraudulent or deceptive purposes. Spammers, scammers, and misinformation campaigns often exploit known weaknesses in algorithms to increase their visibility or bypass content moderation filters. Companies must navigate the fine line between providing transparency and preventing exploitation, ensuring that openness does not lead to further algorithmic abuse.

The push for algorithm transparency is likely to continue as AI systems become more embedded in daily life. Whether in social media, search engines, financial services, or healthcare, the demand for clear, explainable, and accountable algorithms will shape the future of digital regulation. Governments, researchers, and industry leaders must work together to establish standards that promote transparency while balancing innovation and security. Understanding what algorithms do and how they shape the digital world is essential for ensuring that they serve the public interest rather than reinforcing hidden biases, misinformation, and corporate agendas.

The Dangers of Algorithmic Addiction

Social media platforms, video streaming services, and digital marketplaces have transformed the way people consume content, engage with others, and interact with technology. At the heart of this transformation lies the power of algorithms—sophisticated machine learning systems designed to capture and maintain user attention. These algorithms dictate what people see, how often they see it, and how they engage with digital platforms. While their primary purpose is to enhance user experience and keep engagement high, they have also contributed to a growing problem known as algorithmic addiction. This phenomenon occurs when users become trapped in compulsive digital behaviors, repeatedly engaging with content in ways that are difficult to control. The dangers of algorithmic addiction extend beyond excessive screen time, influencing mental health, productivity, decision-making, and even social interactions.

One of the primary drivers of algorithmic addiction is the way recommendation systems are designed. Platforms such as TikTok, Instagram, YouTube, and Facebook use machine learning to analyze user behavior and predict what content will keep them engaged the longest. These systems track every interaction—likes, comments, shares, watch time, and even scrolling speed—to refine their predictions and serve increasingly personalized content. The more a user interacts with specific types of content, the better the algorithm becomes at keeping them engaged. This creates an endless feedback loop where users are continuously exposed to content that aligns with their interests and emotional triggers, making it difficult to disengage.

Infinite scrolling and autoplay features further reinforce algorithmic addiction by removing natural stopping points. Unlike traditional media formats, where users actively choose when to start and stop consuming content, digital platforms are designed to eliminate these boundaries. Infinite scrolling ensures that users are always presented with something new, preventing them from reaching a logical stopping point. Autoplay features on platforms like YouTube and Netflix seamlessly transition users to the next video, reducing the likelihood of disengagement. These mechanisms exploit cognitive tendencies that make it difficult for individuals to resist consuming more content, leading to prolonged screen time and reduced self-control over digital consumption.

The gamification of engagement is another significant factor contributing to algorithmic addiction. Many platforms incorporate features such as likes, comments, shares, streaks, and badges to create a sense of achievement and reward. These mechanisms tap into psychological principles of reinforcement, where users experience a dopamine release when they receive digital validation. Social media apps, in particular, encourage users to seek approval through engagement metrics, making them more likely to return frequently to check for new interactions. This cycle of instant gratification can lead to compulsive behaviors, where users continuously seek engagement-driven rewards at the expense of real-world activities and relationships.

Algorithmic addiction has profound implications for mental health. Studies have shown that excessive social media and digital content consumption are linked to increased anxiety, depression, and loneliness. Users who spend hours scrolling through algorithmically curated feeds often compare themselves to idealized representations of others, leading to negative self-perception and diminished self-esteem. The constant exposure to curated, highly engaging content can distort reality, making everyday life seem less exciting or meaningful in comparison. Additionally, the endless stream of algorithm-driven content can contribute to information overload, making it difficult for individuals to process and retain meaningful information, leading to increased stress and cognitive fatigue.

The impact of algorithmic addiction extends beyond mental health, affecting productivity and focus. Digital platforms are designed to capture attention, making it challenging for users to concentrate on tasks that require sustained effort. The frequent interruptions caused by social media notifications, algorithm-driven content recommendations, and real-time engagement metrics fragment attention spans, reducing the ability to engage in deep work. Many individuals find themselves repeatedly checking their phones or refreshing feeds, even when they have no real intention of doing so. This compulsive behavior diminishes workplace efficiency, academic performance, and overall cognitive function, leading to decreased productivity in professional and personal life.

Algorithmic addiction also affects social interactions and relationships. The need to stay constantly engaged with digital content can lead to reduced face-to-face interactions and diminished social skills. People may prioritize online engagement over in-person conversations, leading to weaker interpersonal connections and increased social isolation. The addictive nature of algorithm-driven platforms can cause individuals to withdraw from real-world activities, substituting genuine human experiences with digital interactions that provide instant but often shallow gratification. This shift in social behavior has raised concerns about the long-term effects of digital addiction on emotional intelligence, empathy, and the ability to form meaningful relationships.

Children and adolescents are particularly vulnerable to algorithmic addiction. Younger users are still developing self-regulation skills, making them more susceptible to the persuasive techniques used by digital platforms. Social media apps, gaming platforms, and video-sharing sites are specifically designed to maximize engagement among younger audiences, often leading to excessive screen time and reduced participation in physical activities, schoolwork, and family interactions. Studies have indicated that children who spend excessive time on algorithm-driven platforms are more likely to experience sleep disturbances, behavioral issues, and academic struggles. The lack of parental controls and algorithmic transparency makes it difficult for caregivers to regulate their children's digital consumption effectively.

Despite growing awareness of algorithmic addiction, tech companies have little incentive to change their engagement-driven models. Digital platforms generate revenue through advertisements, which means their profitability is directly tied to keeping users on their apps for as long as possible. The more time users spend engaging with algorithm-driven content, the more data is collected, allowing for more precise ad targeting and increased ad revenue. This business model creates a conflict of interest, as companies prioritize user engagement over well-being. While some platforms have introduced features such as screen time tracking, digital well-being tools, and content reminders, these measures often serve as superficial solutions that do not address the core issue of algorithmic persuasion.

Regulatory efforts to combat algorithmic addiction are gaining traction, with policymakers considering measures to hold tech companies accountable for the addictive nature of their platforms. Some governments have proposed laws requiring platforms to provide greater transparency about how their algorithms operate and how they influence user behavior. Other proposals include restrictions on autoplay features, limits on engagement-driven notifications, and mandates for ethical AI design that prioritizes user well-being over profit. While these efforts represent progress, implementing effective regulation remains challenging due to the global nature of digital platforms and the rapid evolution of AI-driven recommendation systems.

The fight against algorithmic addiction ultimately requires a combination of personal awareness, industry responsibility, and policy intervention. Users must take active steps to regain control over their digital consumption, such as setting screen time limits, turning off unnecessary notifications, and engaging in offline activities that promote well-being. Digital literacy programs can help individuals recognize the persuasive techniques used by algorithms and develop healthier online habits. At the same time, tech companies must acknowledge their role in creating addictive systems and take meaningful steps to prioritize ethical design, transparency, and user control. Governments and regulatory bodies must continue pushing for accountability, ensuring that digital platforms do not exploit human psychology for profit at the expense of mental health and well-being.

As algorithmic systems become even more sophisticated, the dangers of algorithmic addiction will continue to evolve. The challenge is not just about reducing screen time but about creating a digital environment where users have greater control over their online experiences, free from manipulative engagement tactics. Recognizing the impact of algorithm-driven behavior and taking proactive measures to address it is essential in shaping a healthier and more balanced relationship with technology.

Algorithmic Recommendations vs. Human Choice

Algorithmic recommendation systems have become an integral part of the digital experience, shaping what people watch, read, listen to, and purchase. From social media feeds and streaming services to online shopping and news aggregation, artificial intelligence determines what content is presented to users based on their past behavior and predicted preferences. These systems promise convenience, personalization, and efficiency, making it easier for people to discover new content without actively searching for it. However, the rise of algorithmic recommendations has raised concerns about the erosion of human choice, as individuals increasingly rely on automated suggestions rather than independent decision-making. The balance between algorithmic curation and human autonomy is a growing debate, with implications for information access, consumer behavior, and even cognitive development.

One of the key advantages of algorithmic recommendations is their ability to personalize content at scale. Platforms like Netflix, YouTube, and Spotify use machine learning to analyze user interactions, identifying patterns in viewing, listening, and browsing history. This allows them to generate recommendations tailored to individual preferences, eliminating the need for users to sift through vast libraries of content manually. Instead of spending time searching for a movie or song, users are presented with curated lists designed to match their tastes. While this enhances convenience, it also means that much of what people consume is shaped by an algorithm rather than an active, deliberate choice.

The same principle applies to news consumption, where recommendation algorithms determine which articles appear in search results, social media feeds, and news aggregator apps. Google News, Apple News, and Facebook's news feed use AI-driven ranking systems to prioritize content based on relevance, engagement history, and user interests. This system ensures that people receive news that aligns with their existing preferences, but it also raises concerns about filter bubbles and echo chambers. When individuals are repeatedly exposed to information that reinforces their beliefs, they may become less likely to seek out diverse perspectives, reducing critical thinking and increasing ideological polarization.

Algorithmic recommendations also influence consumer behavior in online shopping. E-commerce platforms such as Amazon and eBay use AI-powered systems to suggest products based on browsing history, past purchases, and user demographics. This targeted approach improves the shopping experience by surfacing relevant items, increasing the likelihood of purchase. However, it also narrows consumer choice by steering users toward a limited selection of products rather than allowing them to explore the full range of available options. The recommendations users receive are based on what the algorithm predicts they want, not necessarily what they might choose if given full visibility into the marketplace.

The psychological impact of algorithmic recommendations extends beyond convenience and commerce, affecting how people engage with information and make decisions. When users rely heavily on automated suggestions, they may become less inclined to explore new ideas, challenge their assumptions, or engage in independent research. This phenomenon is particularly concerning in areas such as political discourse, where algorithmic content curation can reinforce biases rather than expose individuals to different viewpoints. The more users interact with algorithmically curated content, the more their digital environment is shaped by machine learning predictions rather than conscious human choices.

There is also the issue of serendipity—the ability to discover something unexpected or stumble upon new interests organically. Before algorithmic recommendations dominated digital interactions, people often found books, music, or films through personal exploration, social interactions, or browsing physical stores. This process encouraged curiosity and spontaneous discovery, allowing individuals to develop unique tastes and perspectives. In contrast, algorithmic recommendations prioritize familiarity over novelty, frequently suggesting content that aligns with past behaviors rather than encouraging exploration. While some platforms attempt to introduce variety by suggesting trending content or highlighting diverse options, the core mechanism of recommendation systems remains focused on predicting and reinforcing user preferences.

Despite these concerns, algorithmic recommendations are not inherently negative. They provide immense value by helping users navigate overwhelming amounts of content, saving time, and offering personalized experiences. Many people appreciate the ability to receive tailored suggestions without having to manually search for content that aligns with their interests. However, the challenge lies in ensuring that these systems enhance rather than replace human choice. Users should have more control over their recommendation settings, with options to adjust algorithmic priorities, expand content diversity, or opt for manual browsing when desired.

One potential solution is the development of hybrid models that combine algorithmic recommendations with human agency. Some platforms have introduced features that allow users to toggle between automated suggestions and chronological or manually curated feeds. Others offer customization tools that enable individuals to adjust content preferences, filter recommendation sources, or set exposure limits for specific topics. These approaches help maintain the benefits of AI-driven personalization while preserving user autonomy and decision-making.

Transparency in how recommendation algorithms operate is also crucial for maintaining trust and ensuring informed user interactions. Many platforms do not disclose the exact criteria used to generate recommendations, making it difficult for users to understand why they are being shown certain content. Providing more insight into the mechanics of recommendation systems—such as indicating why a particular suggestion appears, offering alternative content options, or allowing users to modify ranking factors—can help empower individuals to make more intentional choices.

Regulatory efforts are beginning to address the influence of algorithmic recommendations on consumer behavior, digital well-being, and information access. Policymakers have proposed laws requiring platforms to disclose how their recommendation algorithms work and to give users greater control over content curation. Some regulations focus on preventing manipulative algorithmic practices, such as dark patterns that push users toward specific actions or engagement-driven systems that prioritize sensationalist content over accuracy. While regulation alone cannot solve the challenges of algorithmic influence, it represents a step toward greater accountability and user empowerment.

As artificial intelligence continues to advance, the relationship between algorithmic recommendations and human choice will remain a critical area of discussion. The goal should not be to eliminate algorithmic curation but to ensure that it serves as an aid rather than a replacement for independent decision-making. Digital platforms must prioritize ethical design, providing users with the tools to balance automated recommendations with personal exploration. Encouraging algorithmic diversity, promoting digital literacy, and fostering awareness of how recommendation systems shape online behavior can help individuals maintain agency in an increasingly AI-driven world.

The future of content discovery will likely involve a blend of algorithmic intelligence and human intuition. While recommendation systems will continue to play a central role in shaping digital experiences, there must be a conscious effort to preserve the elements of choice, exploration, and serendipity that define meaningful engagement with information and culture. Recognizing the distinction between algorithmic suggestions and genuine human choice is essential in navigating the complexities of digital consumption and ensuring that technology remains a tool for empowerment rather than passive influence.

The Hidden Costs of Social Media Algorithms

Social media algorithms shape the way people consume information, interact with content, and engage with others online. These complex systems are designed to optimize engagement, ensuring that users stay on platforms for as long as possible. While algorithms provide personalized experiences and convenience, they also come with hidden costs that impact mental health, privacy, democracy, and societal well-being. These costs are often overlooked because the benefits of algorithmic curation—tailored recommendations, seamless navigation, and real-time updates—are immediate and visible. However, the long-term consequences of algorithm-driven social media raise concerns about the ethical, psychological, and structural impacts these systems have on individuals and society as a whole.

One of the most significant hidden costs of social media algorithms is their effect on mental health. Platforms are designed to maximize engagement by promoting content that triggers emotional reactions. Studies have shown that social media algorithms prioritize posts that evoke strong emotions, such as outrage, excitement, or sadness, because these emotions increase user interaction. While this keeps users engaged, it also fosters anxiety, stress, and polarization. The constant exposure to algorithmically curated content can distort perceptions of reality, making users feel that the world is more chaotic, divisive, or dangerous than it actually is. In addition, algorithms encourage social comparison by amplifying idealized images, lifestyles, and achievements, leading to feelings of inadequacy, low self-esteem, and depression.

Another hidden cost is the loss of privacy. Social media algorithms rely on extensive data collection to refine their predictions and personalize content. Every interaction, from likes and shares to scrolling behavior and time spent on posts, is tracked and analyzed to create detailed user profiles. These profiles are used to deliver highly targeted advertisements and recommendations, but they also expose users to data exploitation and security risks. Platforms monetize user data by selling it to advertisers and third-party companies, often without clear consent or transparency. Data breaches and leaks further highlight the risks associated with algorithm-driven platforms, as personal information can be accessed, stolen, or misused.

The spread of misinformation and manipulation is another consequence of algorithmic social media. Because engagement-driven algorithms prioritize sensational and emotionally charged content, misinformation often spreads faster than factual news. False stories, conspiracy theories, and misleading narratives can gain traction quickly, influencing public opinion, political discourse, and even election outcomes. Bad actors, including foreign governments and interest groups, exploit algorithmic vulnerabilities to manipulate users and push specific agendas. Social media algorithms do not differentiate between accurate and misleading information; they simply amplify what generates the most engagement. This creates an environment where misinformation thrives, eroding trust in institutions, science, and journalism.

The economic costs of algorithmic social media extend beyond advertising profits for platforms. Businesses, content creators, and media outlets that rely on social media for visibility are at the mercy of algorithmic changes. Platforms frequently adjust their ranking systems, often deprioritizing certain types of content while promoting others. These changes can have devastating effects on small businesses, independent creators, and news organizations that depend on social media traffic. Many companies and individuals invest time and resources into growing their online presence, only to see their reach diminished overnight due to an algorithmic shift. This unpredictable landscape forces businesses to continuously adapt, often at great financial and strategic cost.

The influence of algorithms on democracy and political engagement is another hidden cost. Social media has become a primary source of political information, but algorithms filter and curate content based on what they predict users will engage with most. This leads to filter bubbles, where individuals are exposed only to viewpoints that align with their existing beliefs. As a result, political discourse becomes more fragmented, and ideological divisions deepen. Algorithms do not promote balanced or nuanced discussions; they amplify the most engaging and emotionally charged content, often favoring extreme opinions over rational debate. This dynamic has contributed to the rise of political polarization, misinformation campaigns, and distrust in democratic institutions.

The addictive nature of algorithmic social media is another cost that affects both individuals and society. Platforms use AI-driven engagement tactics, such as infinite scrolling, autoplay, and notification alerts, to keep users engaged for as long as possible. The more time users spend on a platform, the more data is collected, and the more advertising revenue is generated. However, this business model encourages compulsive behavior, leading to excessive screen time, distraction, and reduced productivity. Many users struggle to limit their social media use, experiencing withdrawal symptoms when they attempt to take breaks. This addiction-like behavior has led to concerns about digital well-being, particularly among younger users who are more susceptible to algorithmic reinforcement loops.

The environmental impact of algorithmic social media is another hidden cost that is rarely discussed. The data centers that power social media platforms require enormous amounts of energy to process, store, and deliver algorithmically curated content. The carbon footprint of digital consumption continues to grow as more users engage with video content, live streaming, and high-resolution media. Algorithm-driven engagement maximizes content consumption, encouraging users to stream videos, browse endlessly, and generate massive amounts of digital waste. While the focus is often on individual energy consumption, the larger issue is the infrastructure that supports algorithmic social media, which contributes to the overall demand for energy-intensive computing resources.

The ethical considerations of algorithm-driven social media cannot be ignored. While platforms justify algorithmic curation as a way to enhance user experience, the underlying goal is to maximize engagement and advertising revenue. This prioritization of profit over user well-being raises ethical questions about the responsibility of social media companies. Should platforms be held accountable for the mental health impacts of their algorithms? Should they be required to limit data collection and provide greater transparency? These questions highlight the broader debate about the role of technology in society and the need for stronger oversight and ethical AI design.

Efforts to address the hidden costs of social media algorithms have gained traction, but challenges remain. Some platforms have introduced features such as screen time tracking, content moderation improvements, and misinformation warnings. However, these efforts often serve as partial solutions rather than systemic changes. Regulatory discussions have focused on algorithmic transparency, requiring platforms to disclose how their recommendation systems work and how they influence content visibility. Some governments have proposed stricter data privacy laws to limit the exploitation of user data, while others have considered legal action against platforms that fail to prevent the spread of harmful content. While regulation is an important step, social media companies continue to resist measures that could reduce their profitability.

The responsibility to address the hidden costs of social media algorithms does not fall solely on governments and tech companies. Users also play a role in understanding how these systems affect their lives and taking proactive steps to mitigate negative impacts. Developing digital literacy skills, being mindful of engagement habits, questioning information sources, and setting personal boundaries for social media use can help individuals regain control over their digital experiences. Educators, researchers, and advocacy groups must continue to raise awareness about algorithmic influence, ensuring that people have the knowledge and tools to navigate social media critically.

The hidden costs of social media algorithms are vast, affecting mental health, privacy, democracy, the economy, and even the environment. While algorithms offer convenience and personalization, their long-term consequences cannot be ignored. Addressing these issues requires a combination of regulatory action, ethical technology development, and user awareness. The future of social media will depend on how these challenges are managed and whether platforms, policymakers, and users can work together to create a digital ecosystem that prioritizes well-being, fairness, and accountability over engagement-driven profit.

How to Navigate Social Media Without Falling for Algorithmic Traps

Social media platforms are designed to capture attention, encourage engagement, and maximize the time users spend interacting with content. Behind every like, share, and comment, there are powerful algorithms that shape the digital experience, determining what content appears in feeds, what videos are recommended, and which topics gain visibility. While these systems provide convenience and personalization, they also create algorithmic traps that can manipulate behavior, limit exposure to diverse perspectives, and encourage compulsive usage. Navigating social media without falling for these traps requires awareness, critical thinking, and intentional digital habits.

One of the first steps in avoiding algorithmic manipulation is understanding how social media platforms operate. Every platform, whether it is Facebook, Instagram, Twitter, TikTok, or YouTube, uses machine learning to analyze user behavior and optimize content recommendations. The primary goal of these algorithms is to maximize engagement, which often means prioritizing content that triggers strong emotional responses. Posts that spark outrage, excitement, or curiosity tend to be amplified because they generate more interactions. Recognizing that algorithms are not neutral but rather designed to keep users engaged can help in making more conscious decisions about digital consumption.

Personalization is one of the most powerful features of algorithm-driven platforms, but it also creates echo chambers that reinforce existing beliefs and preferences. When users consistently engage with certain types of content, the algorithm learns to prioritize similar material, reducing exposure to different viewpoints. This can lead to intellectual isolation, where users only see information that aligns with their biases while opposing perspectives become invisible. Breaking free from this cycle requires intentional efforts to seek out diverse perspectives. Following a variety of sources, engaging with content that challenges assumptions, and manually searching for information outside of algorithmic recommendations can help counteract the effects of personalization.

Another common algorithmic trap is the endless scrolling feature that keeps users engaged for prolonged periods. Platforms like Instagram, TikTok, and Twitter are designed to provide an uninterrupted stream of content, making it easy to lose track of time. The more users scroll, the more data algorithms collect, further refining their ability to predict what will keep them engaged. Setting time limits for social media use, using productivity apps to track screen time, and establishing intentional browsing habits can help avoid the compulsion to scroll indefinitely. Taking regular breaks and setting specific timeframes for social media consumption can reduce algorithm-driven distraction.

Notifications are another tool used by platforms to reinforce habitual engagement. Every like, comment, and message notification serves as a digital trigger, prompting users to return to the platform and interact with content. These notifications create a sense of urgency, making users feel as though they must respond immediately. Disabling non-essential notifications, turning off app alerts, and customizing notification settings can help reduce digital distractions and prevent social media from dictating attention. Checking platforms at designated times rather than reacting to notifications in real-time allows for greater control over digital interactions.

Clickbait and sensationalized content are other algorithmic traps designed to capture attention and drive engagement. Many posts, articles, and videos use exaggerated headlines, misleading thumbnails, or emotionally charged language to entice users into clicking. The more engagement these types of posts receive, the more they are amplified by algorithms. Avoiding clickbait involves developing critical media literacy skills, questioning the credibility of sources, and being mindful of content designed to manipulate emotions. Fact-checking information before sharing it and seeking out primary sources rather than relying on algorithmically promoted content can help in navigating social media responsibly.

Another challenge posed by social media algorithms is the tendency to amplify extreme content. Since outrage and controversy generate high levels of engagement, divisive posts often receive more visibility than nuanced discussions. This can create a distorted perception of reality, making the world seem more polarized than it actually is. Engaging with constructive discussions, avoiding reactionary content, and being mindful of how engagement patterns shape feeds can help counteract the negative effects of algorithm-driven polarization. Choosing to interact with balanced, well-researched content instead of emotionally manipulative posts contributes to a healthier digital environment.

Algorithmic advertising is another area where users must be cautious. Platforms track browsing habits, online purchases, and engagement history to deliver highly targeted ads. These ads are designed to be seamless, often blending into regular content and making it difficult to distinguish between organic posts and paid promotions. Being aware of how data is used for targeted advertising can help in making more informed choices. Reviewing privacy settings, opting out of personalized ads when possible, and being mindful of impulse-driven purchases influenced by algorithmic targeting can reduce the impact of algorithm-driven consumer manipulation.

Social media addiction is a growing concern, as platforms use AI-driven engagement techniques to keep users online for as long as possible. Features such as autoplay, suggested videos, and real-time content updates encourage continuous engagement, making it difficult to disconnect. Developing healthier digital habits involves setting boundaries, prioritizing offline activities, and using social media with intention rather than out of compulsion. Practicing digital mindfulness—such as being aware of emotional responses to content, setting clear goals for social media use, and engaging in meaningful interactions rather than passive consumption—can improve the quality of online experiences.

Another way to navigate social media more effectively is by customizing algorithmic settings whenever possible. Some platforms allow users to adjust feed preferences, switch to chronological timelines, or limit certain types of content recommendations. Taking advantage of these features can provide more control over the digital experience. Actively curating follow lists, muting or unfollowing accounts that contribute to negative digital habits, and using features that allow for manual content discovery rather than algorithmic recommendations can help in maintaining a healthier relationship with social media.

Engaging with social media consciously also involves being aware of how content is monetized. Platforms thrive on ad revenue, influencer marketing, and paid promotions, which influence what is prioritized in feeds. Recognizing the financial incentives behind algorithmic decisions can help in making more intentional choices about what to consume and support. Following independent content creators, supporting platforms that prioritize transparency, and seeking out alternative information sources can contribute to a more balanced digital experience.

Educational initiatives focused on digital literacy can also play a crucial role in helping users navigate algorithmic traps. Understanding how social media algorithms function, recognizing engagement-driven content strategies, and learning about data privacy can empower users to make informed decisions. Encouraging critical thinking, questioning the motives behind viral trends, and being skeptical of algorithmic influence can help users maintain autonomy in their digital interactions.

Social media is a powerful tool for communication, information, and entertainment, but its algorithmic foundations are designed to shape behavior in ways that are not always in users' best interests. Awareness, intentionality, and critical engagement are essential for navigating social media without falling for algorithmic traps. By taking control of digital consumption, diversifying content sources, and practicing mindful engagement, users can create a healthier and more balanced relationship with social media while minimizing the negative effects of algorithm-driven manipulation.

The Future of AI-Driven Social Media Experiences

Artificial intelligence is rapidly transforming the way people interact with social media, shaping the content they see, the way they communicate, and how platforms evolve. AI-driven social media experiences are becoming more personalized, immersive, and predictive, changing the nature of digital engagement. As machine learning models become more advanced, social media platforms will continue refining their algorithms to maximize user retention, content relevance, and advertising efficiency. These changes will bring both opportunities and challenges, raising important questions about privacy, autonomy, misinformation, and digital well-being.

One of the most significant advancements in AI-driven social media experiences is the increasing level of personalization. Algorithms already curate content based on user behavior, but future AI models will refine recommendations with even greater precision. Platforms will analyze not only what users engage with but also their emotional responses, facial expressions, voice tones, and even biometric data. These systems will learn to predict moods and tailor content accordingly, creating an experience that feels more intuitive and engaging. While this may enhance user satisfaction, it also raises concerns about emotional manipulation, as platforms could exploit subconscious reactions to keep users engaged longer.

Conversational AI and virtual influencers are expected to play a larger role in social media interactions. AI-generated avatars, chatbots, and synthetic personalities will become more lifelike, making digital interactions feel increasingly human. These AI-powered influencers will engage with users in real time, responding to comments, generating personalized messages, and even adapting their personalities based on user preferences. Some brands have already experimented with AI influencers, but future advancements will blur the line between artificial and human content creation. As these AI-driven personas gain influence, ethical concerns about authenticity, transparency, and trust will become more pressing.

The evolution of generative AI will also impact content creation on social media. AI models will assist users in producing high-quality images, videos, and text with minimal effort. Automated content generators will enable users to create professional-looking posts, write compelling captions, and enhance visual aesthetics instantly. AI-assisted creativity will lower the barriers to content production, making it easier for individuals and businesses to maintain an online presence. However, this could lead to an oversaturation of AI-generated content, making it more difficult to distinguish between human-created and machine-generated material. The rise of deepfake technology will further complicate this landscape, as AI-generated videos and voice clones become more realistic and harder to detect.

Social media engagement metrics will become increasingly sophisticated as AI systems analyze more granular aspects of user interactions. Instead of relying solely on likes, shares, and comments, platforms will track micro-expressions, eye movements, scrolling behavior, and engagement depth. These data points will be used to fine-tune content recommendations, optimizing feeds for maximum attention. AI will predict when users are most likely to engage and adjust content delivery schedules accordingly. While this will make social media experiences feel more seamless and intuitive, it could also deepen addictive behaviors, reinforcing algorithmic dependency and reducing users' ability to control their digital consumption.

AI-driven moderation will play a critical role in shaping the future of social media. Current moderation tools struggle to detect context, nuance, and intent in online conversations, leading to inconsistent content enforcement. Future AI models will be better equipped to interpret meaning, identifying hate speech, misinformation, and harmful content with greater accuracy. AI moderation will reduce the reliance on human moderators, automating the process of flagging and removing problematic posts. However, challenges remain in ensuring that these systems do not suppress free speech or misinterpret cultural nuances. AI bias in moderation algorithms could disproportionately affect certain communities, highlighting the need for transparency and oversight in automated decision-making.

The integration of AI into augmented reality and virtual reality will redefine social media experiences, making digital interactions more immersive. The development of the metaverse, a fully interactive virtual space powered by AI, will create new social environments where users can engage in real-time conversations, attend events, and share experiences in ways that go beyond traditional social media formats. AI-driven avatars will facilitate more dynamic interactions, personalizing virtual spaces based on user preferences. This shift will transform how people socialize online, merging digital and physical realities in ways that were once considered science fiction.

AI-powered predictive analytics will reshape advertising strategies on social media. Instead of simply targeting users based on demographics and interests, future AI models will anticipate consumer needs before users even express them. Advanced AI will predict purchasing intent based on behavioral patterns, past interactions, and external factors such as location, weather, and mood. This hyper-targeted approach will make advertising more effective, but it will also raise concerns about data privacy and consumer manipulation. Users may find themselves receiving product recommendations based on subconscious cues they were unaware they had provided, further reducing their autonomy in decision-making.

The role of AI in misinformation detection and content credibility will become increasingly important. As misinformation spreads more rapidly through algorithmic amplification, AI-driven fact-checking tools will be developed to counteract false narratives. These systems will analyze sources, detect inconsistencies, and flag misleading content in real time. Some platforms will introduce AI-assisted content verification, allowing users to see automated credibility scores for articles and posts. While this could help combat misinformation, the challenge will be ensuring that AI-driven fact-checking remains unbiased and free from corporate or political influence.

AI will also enhance accessibility in social media, making digital platforms more inclusive for people with disabilities. AI-powered speech-to-text and text-to-speech tools will improve communication for users with hearing or vision impairments. Gesture-based interfaces and brain-computer integration could further enhance accessibility, enabling users to interact with social media through new forms of input. AI-driven translation tools will break down language barriers, making global communication more seamless. These advancements will contribute to a more inclusive digital landscape, allowing more people to participate in online communities.

The future of AI-driven social media will also be shaped by regulatory and ethical considerations. Governments and advocacy groups will push for greater algorithmic transparency, requiring platforms to disclose how AI models operate and what data they collect. There will be increased scrutiny over AI biases, content manipulation, and digital addiction, prompting discussions about ethical AI design. Some countries may introduce laws limiting the extent to which AI can personalize content, ensuring that users have more control over their digital experiences. As public awareness of algorithmic influence grows, demand for user agency in AI-driven platforms will increase.

As AI continues to evolve, the social media landscape will shift in ways that are both exciting and concerning. The potential for more personalized, immersive, and predictive experiences will redefine digital engagement, but the ethical challenges of AI-driven influence cannot be ignored. Striking a balance between innovation and responsibility will be crucial in shaping the future of social media. The decisions made today regarding AI transparency, algorithmic accountability, and digital well-being will determine whether social media enhances human connection or deepens algorithmic dependency. The future of AI-driven social media experiences will not be shaped by technology alone but by the choices that users, developers, and policymakers make in navigating this rapidly evolving digital ecosystem.

Breaking Free: How to Take Control of Your Digital Experience

Social media platforms, search engines, and digital services have become an inseparable part of daily life, shaping the way people interact, consume information, and make decisions. While these platforms offer convenience, entertainment, and connection, they are also designed to maximize engagement, often leading to excessive screen time, algorithmic manipulation, and digital dependency. Many users find themselves trapped in cycles of compulsive scrolling, passive content consumption, and constant notifications, making it difficult to maintain control over their digital experiences. Taking back control requires awareness, intentionality, and a commitment to reshaping online habits in a way that aligns with personal well-being rather than algorithmic design.

One of the first steps in regaining control over the digital experience is recognizing how algorithms influence online behavior. Social media feeds, search results, and video recommendations are not neutral; they are curated by machine learning models that prioritize engagement over user autonomy. Every click, like, share, and comment informs the algorithm about preferences, reinforcing patterns that dictate what appears on the screen. Understanding this dynamic allows users to make more conscious choices about how they interact with digital platforms. Being aware of the forces shaping online experiences makes it easier to step back and evaluate whether digital consumption aligns with personal goals and values.

Customizing platform settings is an effective way to disrupt algorithmic control. Many social media networks and digital services offer options to adjust recommendation preferences, disable autoplay, and switch to chronological feeds. These small changes reduce the passive consumption of algorithmically curated content, giving users more control over what they see and when they see it. Disabling personalized ads, opting out of data tracking, and restricting third-party app permissions further limits how much information is collected and used for targeted engagement. Exploring privacy settings and making intentional adjustments can significantly alter how digital platforms interact with personal data.

Breaking free from compulsive social media use requires setting clear boundaries and time limits. Many people find themselves checking their phones instinctively, often without realizing how much time they spend scrolling through feeds or watching algorithm-driven videos. Using built-in screen time monitoring tools, setting app usage limits, and scheduling device-free periods throughout the day can help reduce excessive engagement. Establishing designated times for checking notifications, responding to messages, and consuming content prevents platforms from dictating attention and focus. Practicing intentional screen use makes digital interactions more purposeful and less driven by habit or algorithmic reinforcement.

Notifications are one of the most powerful tools used by digital platforms to maintain user engagement. Every like, comment, and update serves as a psychological trigger, prompting users to return to the app and continue interacting. Disabling non-essential notifications, muting group chats, and customizing alert settings can reduce the constant interruptions that disrupt concentration and fuel digital dependency. Checking notifications at specific times rather than reacting instantly allows users to regain control over their attention. Creating tech-free zones, such as keeping phones out of the bedroom or limiting device use during meals, also helps establish healthier digital habits.

Diversifying information sources is another key strategy for taking control of digital experiences. Algorithms often create filter bubbles, where users are repeatedly exposed to content that aligns with their existing preferences and beliefs. Expanding media consumption beyond algorithmic recommendations ensures a broader and more balanced perspective. Following diverse news sources, exploring different viewpoints, and manually searching for information rather than relying on curated feeds prevents algorithmic reinforcement of biases. Engaging with high-quality, well-researched content rather than sensationalist headlines or emotionally charged posts reduces susceptibility to misinformation and digital manipulation.

Mindful content consumption is essential for breaking free from passive engagement. Social media and digital platforms are designed to keep users scrolling, watching, and clicking for as long as possible. Developing awareness of consumption patterns and questioning whether content adds value or simply fills time helps create a more intentional online experience. Before engaging with content, users can ask themselves whether it aligns with personal interests, informs decision-making, or contributes positively to well-being. Unfollowing accounts that promote negativity, comparison, or low-value engagement can improve digital environments and reduce unnecessary distractions.

Reclaiming creativity and productivity in the digital space shifts the role of technology from passive consumption to active creation. Many digital tools can be used for personal growth, learning, and creative expression rather than just entertainment and social validation. Using technology for skill-building, creative projects, and meaningful communication fosters a more enriching relationship with digital platforms. Engaging in activities such as writing, photography, coding, music production, or online learning transforms technology into a tool for self-improvement rather than just a source of passive engagement. Prioritizing meaningful digital interactions over algorithm-driven entertainment reduces reliance on engagement-maximizing platforms.

Developing digital mindfulness helps users recognize emotional responses to online experiences. Algorithms often prioritize content that triggers strong emotions, whether excitement, outrage, or anxiety. Noticing how digital interactions affect mood, stress levels, and mental clarity creates an opportunity to adjust habits accordingly. If social media leaves users feeling drained, unproductive, or emotionally overwhelmed, taking breaks, muting certain accounts, or stepping away from platforms entirely may be beneficial. Digital detoxes, whether for a few hours, days, or weeks, help reset online behaviors and create a healthier balance between virtual and real-world interactions.

Strengthening real-world connections reduces the influence of digital platforms on social interactions. While social media facilitates communication, it often replaces deeper, more meaningful face-to-face relationships. Prioritizing in-person interactions, spending time with family and friends without digital distractions, and engaging in offline hobbies helps counterbalance the effects of excessive screen time. The more fulfilling real-life experiences become, the less reliant users feel on algorithm-driven validation and online engagement. Reclaiming time for activities that promote personal growth, social connection, and well-being weakens the hold that digital platforms have on attention and behavior.

Becoming an intentional user of digital platforms shifts control away from algorithms and back to the individual. Setting clear goals for social media use—whether for professional networking, staying informed, or connecting with loved ones—prevents aimless scrolling and algorithmic reinforcement. Engaging with content purposefully, rather than reacting to whatever appears in feeds, creates a more deliberate and meaningful online experience. Users who take an active role in shaping their digital environments are less susceptible to manipulation, digital exhaustion, and compulsive behaviors.

Technology is a tool, and like any tool, its effectiveness depends on how it is used. By developing awareness of algorithmic influence, setting boundaries, and prioritizing intentional engagement, users can regain control over their digital experiences. The goal is not to eliminate social media or digital platforms but to use them in ways that align with personal values, interests, and well-being. Digital freedom comes from making conscious choices about how technology is integrated into daily life, ensuring that it enhances rather than controls human experience.

Can Users Outsmart Social Media Algorithms?

Social media algorithms are designed to maximize engagement, keeping users scrolling, clicking, and interacting for as long as possible. These algorithms use vast amounts of data to predict user behavior, curate personalized content, and ensure that each experience feels tailored to individual preferences. While this optimization creates a seamless digital environment, it also raises concerns about manipulation, loss of autonomy, and algorithmic control over online experiences. Many users wonder whether it is possible to outsmart social media algorithms, breaking free from their influence and regaining control over what they see, how they engage, and how much time they spend online. Outsmarting these algorithms requires a deep understanding of how they work, as well as intentional strategies to disrupt their influence.

One of the most effective ways users can challenge social media algorithms is by disrupting the data patterns that power them. Algorithms rely on consistent behavior to refine recommendations, meaning that every like, share, follow, and click reinforces certain content preferences. By engaging unpredictably, users can confuse the algorithm and prevent it from developing an accurate behavioral model. This might include interacting with a wide range of content, following diverse accounts, and deliberately clicking on posts that do not align with past behaviors. Regularly changing engagement patterns forces the algorithm to reset recommendations, preventing it from trapping users in a cycle of repetitive content.

Actively curating feeds is another way to regain control over the algorithmic experience. Most platforms allow users to adjust content preferences, unfollow accounts, mute certain topics, and prioritize specific types of content. By manually selecting what appears in feeds instead of relying solely on algorithmic curation, users can shape their own digital environments. Taking advantage of chronological feed options, if available, can also help bypass algorithm-driven ranking, ensuring that content appears in real-time rather than being filtered by engagement predictions. While platforms may not always make these customization options easy to find, exploring settings and taking control of content preferences can significantly alter the digital experience.

Limiting engagement with algorithmic traps weakens the influence of social media systems. Clickbait, outrage-driven content, and emotionally charged posts are prioritized because they generate high interaction rates. Avoiding these engagement triggers—such as refusing to comment on divisive posts or ignoring sensational headlines—can reduce the algorithm's ability to manipulate user emotions for increased activity. Instead, engaging with high-quality, meaningful content signals to the algorithm that such material is preferred, shifting recommendations toward more valuable digital interactions.

Another strategy to outsmart algorithms is to use social media with a specific purpose rather than allowing platforms to dictate digital habits. Entering a social media app with an intentional goal—whether to check updates from friends, read news from a trusted source, or engage with a particular community—reduces the likelihood of falling into algorithm-driven engagement loops. Setting time limits, avoiding infinite scrolling, and logging out after completing the intended action prevents platforms from drawing users into extended sessions of passive consumption. Using social media as a tool rather than a default activity helps maintain autonomy over digital interactions.

Disrupting ad targeting mechanisms weakens algorithmic influence over consumer behavior. Social media platforms track browsing history, shopping habits, and content interactions to serve personalized advertisements. Users can limit data collection by disabling ad personalization settings, clearing cookies regularly, and using privacy-focused browsers or VPNs. Engaging with ads in unpredictable ways—such as clicking on irrelevant promotions—can also confuse targeting algorithms, making ad recommendations less precise. Opting out of data tracking wherever possible reduces the ability of social media platforms to tailor marketing efforts based on behavioral analysis.

Following diverse content sources expands the range of information that appears in feeds, challenging algorithmic reinforcement of filter bubbles. Engaging with perspectives outside of personal beliefs, subscribing to independent news outlets, and manually searching for content rather than relying on recommended posts can prevent ideological isolation. Algorithms tend to prioritize content that aligns with past engagement patterns, reinforcing confirmation bias. Intentionally seeking out varied viewpoints disrupts this cycle, ensuring a broader, more balanced digital experience.

Using alternative social media platforms that prioritize transparency and user control offers another way to bypass algorithmic influence. Some decentralized or open-source platforms allow users to customize ranking systems, choose whether to use algorithms at all, and engage without the heavy-handed data collection seen in mainstream networks. Exploring these alternatives provides insight into what social media could look like in a model where users have more agency over their digital experiences. While major platforms dominate online interactions, growing interest in privacy-conscious and user-driven platforms signals a shift toward more ethical social media design.

Developing digital literacy skills strengthens resistance to algorithmic manipulation. Understanding how social media algorithms function, recognizing engagement-driven content strategies, and staying informed about data privacy practices empower users to navigate platforms more critically. The more users understand the mechanics of digital influence, the better they can make intentional choices that align with their own interests rather than being passively shaped by algorithmic design. Digital literacy also includes being aware of how engagement patterns shape feeds, enabling users to take deliberate actions that counteract algorithmic reinforcement.

While users can take steps to outsmart social media algorithms, platforms continuously evolve, adjusting their models to maintain control over digital interactions. As artificial intelligence becomes more advanced, algorithms will incorporate deeper behavioral analysis, real-time adaptation, and predictive engagement techniques. This means that users must remain vigilant, consistently reassessing their strategies and adapting to new algorithmic tactics. Staying informed about changes in social media systems and remaining proactive in digital habits are essential for maintaining long-term autonomy.

Outsmarting social media algorithms is not about completely avoiding them but about using them on one's own terms. By disrupting engagement patterns, customizing feeds, limiting data tracking, and practicing intentional digital habits, users can reduce algorithmic control and regain agency over their online experiences. Social media should serve as a tool for connection, creativity, and information rather than a system designed to exploit attention and manipulate behavior. Taking back control requires continuous effort, but it is possible to navigate social media in a way that prioritizes personal well-being over algorithmic influence.

Open-Source Algorithms and Their Potential Impact

Algorithms dictate much of what happens in the digital world, shaping what users see, interact with, and experience online. From social media feeds to search engine rankings, proprietary algorithms remain at the core of major technology platforms, often operating as black boxes that provide little insight into their mechanics. Users, regulators, and even content creators have limited knowledge of how these systems function, raising concerns about bias, transparency, and accountability. The rise of open-source algorithms presents a potential shift in how algorithms are developed, deployed, and regulated, offering an alternative to the secretive and highly controlled models that dominate the current digital landscape.

Open-source algorithms differ from proprietary ones in that their underlying code is publicly available. This means that developers, researchers, and users can examine, modify, and improve these algorithms. By making code accessible, open-source projects promote transparency, enabling independent audits and reducing the risk of hidden biases. In contrast, proprietary algorithms are closely guarded by corporations, which control how they evolve and operate. The lack of public oversight in proprietary models has led to concerns about algorithmic discrimination, misinformation amplification, and the reinforcement of filter bubbles. Open-source alternatives provide an opportunity to address these challenges while fostering greater public trust in algorithmic decision-making.

One of the most promising aspects of open-source algorithms is their potential to increase fairness in digital systems. Many AI-driven algorithms rely on massive datasets to make decisions, but these datasets often contain biases that go undetected due to the opaque nature of proprietary models. Open-source algorithms allow researchers to scrutinize how decisions are made, identify biases in training data, and propose corrective measures. This level of transparency is essential for ensuring that algorithms do not disproportionately disadvantage certain groups, particularly in areas such as hiring, lending, healthcare, and content moderation. By allowing external experts to assess and refine algorithms, open-source models can contribute to more equitable digital environments.

Another potential impact of open-source algorithms is in enhancing user control over digital experiences. Currently, most users have little say in how recommendation engines shape their feeds, prioritize content, or filter information. Open-source platforms could allow users to customize ranking criteria, adjust content discovery settings, or even choose different algorithmic models based on their preferences. Rather than being at the mercy of opaque engagement-driven algorithms, users could have the option to prioritize chronological feeds, emphasize educational content, or balance exposure to different perspectives. Providing users with greater control over how algorithms function could reduce the negative effects of algorithmic manipulation and digital addiction.

The impact of open-source algorithms extends beyond individual users to developers and smaller tech companies. Large technology firms dominate the digital space in part because they control the most advanced proprietary algorithms. Startups and independent developers often struggle to compete due to the lack of access to similar technology. Open-source algorithms could level the playing field by providing high-quality, publicly available models that developers can use and adapt. This could foster greater competition in the tech industry, reducing the monopolistic power of major corporations while encouraging innovation and ethical AI development.

Content moderation is another area where open-source algorithms could make a significant impact. Social media platforms rely on AI-driven moderation systems to detect and remove harmful content, but these systems often make mistakes, such as flagging legitimate discussions or failing to detect harmful material. The opaque nature of these moderation algorithms makes it difficult to challenge wrongful content removals or understand the reasoning behind enforcement decisions. Open-source moderation algorithms would enable independent audits, ensuring that content moderation policies are applied fairly and consistently. Greater transparency in moderation practices could improve public trust in social media governance, making platforms more accountable to their users.

Open-source algorithms also have the potential to reshape digital advertising. Currently, platforms like Facebook, Google, and Instagram use proprietary algorithms to serve highly targeted ads based on extensive user data collection. This model raises concerns about privacy, as it allows companies to track user behavior, create detailed profiles, and deliver hyper-personalized advertising without clear user consent. Open-source advertising algorithms could introduce more ethical alternatives by providing advertisers with transparent targeting criteria while allowing users to control what personal data is used for ad personalization. If users could opt into or modify ad-targeting parameters, it would create a more balanced relationship between consumers and advertisers, reducing exploitative data practices.

Despite these potential benefits, open-source algorithms also present challenges. One of the biggest concerns is security. Proprietary algorithms, despite their secrecy, benefit from controlled access, reducing the likelihood of malicious actors exploiting their vulnerabilities. Open-source models, while transparent, could be susceptible to manipulation if bad actors identify weaknesses in the system. Developers of open-source algorithms must implement safeguards to prevent abuse, such as adversarial testing, community-driven oversight, and robust security frameworks. Ensuring that open-source models are resistant to exploitation is crucial to maintaining trust in their effectiveness.

Another challenge is the resistance from major technology companies that profit from closed-source algorithms. Many of these companies have built their business models around engagement-driven algorithms that maximize advertising revenue. Opening their algorithms to public scrutiny could expose problematic business practices, reveal biases in ranking systems, and reduce their control over content distribution. While some platforms have taken small steps toward greater transparency—such as publishing limited explanations of how their recommendation engines work—true open-source adoption would require a fundamental shift in how these companies operate. The financial incentives to maintain proprietary control remain strong, making widespread adoption of open-source models unlikely without regulatory pressure or public demand.

Governments and policymakers could play a role in encouraging open-source adoption by introducing legislation that promotes algorithmic transparency. Some jurisdictions have already begun exploring regulations that require platforms to disclose how their algorithms function, particularly in areas such as political advertising, content moderation, and financial decision-making. Open-source models could serve as a regulatory benchmark, providing a framework for how transparent, accountable algorithms should operate. By incentivizing companies to adopt open-source principles or requiring public access to certain algorithmic processes, policymakers could push the tech industry toward greater accountability and ethical AI practices.

The future of open-source algorithms will depend on the willingness of developers, researchers, and policymakers to support transparency in digital systems. While proprietary algorithms will likely continue to dominate the mainstream tech landscape, open-source alternatives offer a vision of a more accountable, user-centered digital ecosystem. As demand for algorithmic transparency grows, open-source models could serve as a powerful counterbalance to corporate-controlled AI, ensuring that algorithmic decision-making prioritizes fairness, privacy, and public interest. The potential impact of open-source algorithms is not just in providing an alternative to proprietary models but in reshaping the way technology interacts with society as a whole.

The Next Generation of AI and Social Media

Artificial intelligence has already transformed the way people interact with social media, but the next generation of AI promises even greater changes. As machine learning models become more sophisticated, they will not only refine content recommendations but also create entirely new ways for users to engage with digital platforms. Social media will move beyond simple algorithms that rank posts based on engagement and evolve into intelligent systems that predict behaviors, generate personalized content, and interact with users in more human-like ways. These advancements will redefine communication, content creation, digital communities, and the ethical concerns surrounding AI-driven platforms.

One of the most significant advancements in AI and social media will be the rise of fully autonomous AI-driven content. Currently, AI assists in generating captions, suggesting hashtags, and recommending videos, but future AI systems will be capable of creating entire social media posts, complete with images, videos, and interactive elements. These AI-generated posts will be indistinguishable from human-created content, making it possible for individuals and brands to automate their online presence completely. Businesses, influencers, and content creators will increasingly rely on AI assistants to generate content, schedule posts, and optimize engagement strategies, reducing the need for manual content creation.

AI-driven chatbots and virtual influencers will also become more advanced, creating a new era of social interaction on digital platforms. These AI personas will be capable of holding conversations that feel natural, responding to messages in real time, and adapting their personalities based on user interactions. Virtual influencers, which already have growing followings on platforms like Instagram and TikTok, will become even more realistic, blurring the line between human and AI-generated social media figures. These virtual personalities will not only entertain but also engage with audiences in meaningful ways, fostering parasocial relationships that feel as real as interactions with human influencers.

The evolution of AI in social media will also change the way users discover and engage with content. Current recommendation systems analyze past behavior to predict what users will find interesting, but next-generation AI will take personalization to an entirely new level. Instead of simply curating content based on engagement history, future AI will predict what users want before they even search for it. This predictive engagement will be powered by advanced behavioral analysis, emotional recognition, and real-time adaptation. AI will analyze facial expressions, tone of voice, and even biometric data to determine mood and deliver content that aligns with a user's emotional state at any given moment.

AI will also transform digital communities by creating intelligent moderation systems that reduce harmful content while promoting meaningful interactions. Current content moderation relies on a combination of automated detection systems and human reviewers, but the next generation of AI will be more capable of understanding context, tone, and nuance. Future AI models will detect hate speech, misinformation, and toxic behavior with greater accuracy, reducing the spread of harmful content while minimizing false positives that remove legitimate discussions. These AI-driven moderation tools will create safer online spaces, ensuring that social media remains a platform for constructive dialogue rather than digital conflict.

Augmented reality and AI-driven social media experiences will merge, creating more immersive interactions. The integration of AI with AR will enable users to engage in real-time, interactive content that goes beyond traditional text and video posts. Virtual hangouts, AI-generated environments, and holographic communication will redefine how people connect online. Social media platforms will shift from being passive content feeds to interactive digital spaces where users can explore AI-generated worlds, attend virtual events, and interact with AI-driven characters. These advancements will change the way people experience digital interactions, making online communities more dynamic and engaging.

AI-powered voice and video synthesis will introduce new forms of content creation and communication. Users will be able to generate realistic AI-driven voiceovers, deepfake-style video alterations, and AI-enhanced storytelling without technical expertise. This will enable entirely new formats of social media engagement, where users can manipulate video content, create AI-generated animations, and produce hyper-personalized multimedia posts. While these tools will unlock creative possibilities, they will also raise ethical concerns about misinformation, as it will become easier to create and distribute highly realistic but entirely fabricated content.

AI-generated news feeds and automated journalism will also reshape the way people consume information on social media. Instead of relying on human editors or traditional news sources, AI-driven algorithms will create custom news reports tailored to each user's interests and preferences. These AI-generated news summaries will be compiled from multiple sources, analyzing vast amounts of information in real time to provide users with highly relevant updates. While this could improve access to personalized news, it may also deepen concerns about filter bubbles, as users may only receive information that reinforces their existing views without exposure to diverse perspectives.

The ethical implications of next-generation AI in social media will become more pressing as these technologies evolve. AI-driven manipulation, digital addiction, and privacy concerns will intensify as platforms become more intelligent in predicting and influencing user behavior. Governments and regulatory bodies will likely implement stricter oversight of AI-driven content generation, algorithmic decision-making, and data collection practices. Transparency in how AI systems function will become a key issue, as users demand greater control over their digital experiences and seek assurances that AI is being used responsibly.

The relationship between humans and AI in social media will also raise philosophical questions about authenticity and digital identity. As AI-generated content, chatbots, and virtual influencers become more common, users may struggle to differentiate between real and artificial interactions. This will create a cultural shift in how people perceive online engagement, forcing a reevaluation of what it means to build genuine connections in a digital landscape increasingly populated by AI-driven entities.

Despite these concerns, the next generation of AI and social media will also bring positive transformations. AI will enable better accessibility features, allowing users with disabilities to engage with content in new ways. Real-time translation, AI-assisted content summarization, and automated transcription services will make social media more inclusive, breaking down language barriers and ensuring that digital platforms are accessible to a global audience. These advancements will empower more people to participate in online conversations and contribute to a more connected world.

As AI continues to shape social media, the challenge will be balancing innovation with ethical considerations. While AI-driven personalization, content generation, and interaction models will enhance user experiences, they will also raise questions about privacy, autonomy, and digital well-being. The next generation of AI in social media will redefine how people communicate, create, and consume content, making it essential for developers, users, and policymakers to navigate these changes thoughtfully. The future of social media will not only be driven by technology but also by the choices people make in shaping how AI is integrated into their digital lives.

Final Thoughts: Where Do We Go from Here?

Social media algorithms have fundamentally reshaped the way people interact with technology, information, and each other. Over the past two decades, platforms have evolved from simple networks for sharing updates into powerful, AI-driven ecosystems that influence public opinion, commerce, entertainment, and even democracy. The growing role of artificial intelligence in content curation, recommendation systems, and engagement strategies has created an environment where user behavior is shaped by invisible forces designed to maximize retention and revenue. While these advancements have brought undeniable benefits, they have also raised ethical, psychological, and societal concerns that demand urgent attention.

The question now is not whether social media algorithms will continue to shape digital experiences, but rather how they will evolve and how society will respond. The future of social media will depend on the balance between innovation and responsibility, between algorithmic efficiency and human agency. Users, developers, policymakers, and regulators all have roles to play in determining whether these systems serve the public good or become mechanisms of control, division, and exploitation. The challenge lies in recognizing the impact of these technologies and ensuring that they are designed and implemented with transparency, fairness, and accountability.

One of the most pressing issues is the question of algorithmic transparency. For years, major tech companies have built their business models around proprietary algorithms that operate as black boxes, making decisions about what users see without clear explanations. Calls for greater transparency have grown louder, with advocates demanding insight into how these systems function, what data they collect, and how they prioritize content. Some companies have begun to offer limited explanations, but true transparency would require independent audits, public disclosure of ranking criteria, and mechanisms that allow users to modify or understand their own algorithmic experiences. Without greater transparency, the power dynamics between tech companies and users will remain lopsided, with control concentrated in the hands of a few corporations.

The role of regulation in shaping the future of social media is another critical factor. Governments and regulatory bodies around the world have started to introduce laws aimed at curbing misinformation, preventing data exploitation, and ensuring that algorithms operate ethically. The European Union's Digital Services Act, for example, places new responsibilities on platforms to assess and mitigate risks associated with algorithmic decision-making. Similar efforts are emerging in the United States and other regions, as lawmakers push for greater oversight of AI-driven systems. However, regulation alone is not a perfect solution. Overregulation could stifle innovation, while poorly designed policies could inadvertently create new challenges, such as excessive content moderation that limits free expression. The key is finding a regulatory balance that promotes ethical AI practices without restricting the positive aspects of digital engagement.

User empowerment is another essential aspect of shaping the future of social media. While companies and governments debate policies, individuals must also take an active role in understanding and managing their digital experiences. Algorithmic awareness should become a fundamental aspect of digital literacy, helping users recognize how their engagement patterns influence what they see. By actively curating feeds, diversifying content sources, and questioning algorithmic recommendations, users can reduce the risk of falling into engagement traps or filter bubbles. Greater control over privacy settings, notification preferences, and content customization will also give individuals more agency in navigating algorithmic environments.

The intersection of AI and social media raises deeper philosophical questions about human agency and digital identity. As algorithms become more advanced, they will not just recommend content but also generate it, blurring the line between human and machine-created interactions. Virtual influencers, AI-generated news articles, and synthetic media will challenge traditional notions of authenticity and trust. Users will need to develop new ways of discerning reality from AI-generated fiction, while platforms must ensure that digital environments do not become dominated by artificial entities that manipulate opinions or reinforce biases. The way people define identity, relationships, and truth in digital spaces will continue to evolve, forcing society to rethink what it means to interact in an AI-driven world.

Economic factors will also shape the next phase of social media development. The current business model of most platforms revolves around engagement-based advertising, where user attention is monetized through targeted ads. This model incentivizes companies to prioritize addictive content, emotional triggers, and data collection. If the economic foundation of social media remains unchanged, many of the problems associated with algorithmic manipulation and privacy violations will persist. Alternative revenue models, such as subscription-based services, decentralized platforms, and ethical advertising frameworks, could offer new ways to sustain social media without relying on hyper-targeted engagement tactics. However, these alternatives must be designed in ways that are accessible and appealing to users, ensuring that ethical digital experiences do not come at the cost of usability or financial exclusivity.

Artificial intelligence will continue to advance, bringing both risks and opportunities. Predictive AI will anticipate user needs before they even express them, creating hyper-personalized experiences that could enhance convenience but also reduce spontaneity and free choice. AI-driven moderation will improve content safety but may introduce new forms of censorship if not carefully implemented. Intelligent automation will revolutionize content creation, making it easier than ever to generate compelling digital media, yet it will also raise ethical concerns about authenticity and authorship. How these technologies are developed and governed will determine whether AI-driven social media becomes a tool for empowerment or a mechanism for control.

The social and cultural impact of algorithms will extend beyond individual platforms, influencing the way people communicate, form opinions, and engage with the world. If algorithms continue to shape political discourse, news consumption, and cultural trends, they will have a profound effect on democratic processes, public trust, and global narratives. Ensuring that these systems promote informed decision-making rather than polarization or misinformation will be a major challenge. The responsibility for addressing these issues does not rest solely with tech companies or regulators but with everyone who participates in the digital ecosystem. A collective effort is required to create an online landscape that prioritizes critical thinking, diverse perspectives, and meaningful connections.

As the future unfolds, the decisions made today about social media algorithms will shape generations to come. Whether users become passive consumers of AI-curated experiences or active participants in shaping ethical digital spaces depends on the awareness, choices, and demands of society. The challenge is not to reject technology but to ensure that it evolves in ways that respect human agency, dignity, and truth. The conversation about algorithmic influence is just beginning, and the path forward will require collaboration, innovation, and a commitment to building a digital world that serves not just corporations and advertisers, but the individuals and communities that rely on it every day.

www.ingramcontent.com/pod-product-compliance
Lightning Source LLC
LaVergne TN
LVHW051229050326
832903LV00028B/2305